THE REBIRTH OF
HISTORY

OLIVIA CONDE

authorHOUSE·

AuthorHouse™ UK
1663 Liberty Drive
Bloomington, IN 47403 USA
www.authorhouse.co.uk
Phone: UK TFN: 0800 0148641 (Toll Free inside the UK)
*   UK Local: (02) 0369 56322 (+44 20 3695 6322 from outside the UK)*

Published by AuthorHouse 10/19/2021

ISBN: 978-1-6655-9394-6 (sc)
ISBN: 978-1-6655-9393-9 (e)

CONTENTS

POEMS OF THE UNIVERSE

The past and present is a small and great step of the grain of the future in the furious flight of waiting hope.

Oblivions sleep with soft gleams on the paths of eternal life.

Cruises open between crosses that raise their flags with free elections.

The endless ending is not lost in the time of the process.

Visions between the invisible whole is theoretical but inseparable at first.

There are flights in dreams for the reason of the universe delivered in body and soul.

The spirits since creation carry the connection with divine harmony.

The colours leave energies from within to welcome the birth of life.

The music leaves between sounds the memories of the outside for the farewell of death.

A circle catches both sides where the inhalation and exhalation exist forever.

Take care of the ladder you climb as it will be the same one you will go down.

I asked at the time what I should do to relieve pain, time answered, let me pass....

PROTESTS AND CLAIMS

They raise their hands the voices shout with posters,
Animal complaints are enthusiastically enforced,
Vaccine heartaches with emotional pain,
Implanted passport leaves the town exhausted,
The ways to oppose are marked as importance,
Behind screens deaf answers are elegant,
Claimants write with beliefs to the target,
The pyramid laughing at the insect that chases it,
Chains are still tied to calm challenges,
Mental alarms watch for the next imbalance,
With more altered steps they launch bigger bullets,
Those in black are not agitated the forbidden is old history,
Signatures go round by hands believing the departure,
The way is wrong from a long time ago,
Feelings do not affect while flock obeys,
The footprints leave most kneeling without strength,
With head high and firm words calm asleep,
From the cold Andes children without education forgotten,
From Africa in misery only amazement observes,
From spiritual india the spiral swallows the system,
From communist china everyone bows their heads,
From Syria to Israel amputations are news,
From Jerusalem three enigmas await the covenant,
From the top the power rejoices seeing the jail,
It is life imprisonment without committing any crime,
The outputs are immense but the principles few,
Prisoners inject themselves with obedience to rules,
They raise firecrackers in the air but the leader is not affected,
The door will not open while the owner is oblivious.

THE SMOKE CURTAIN

The Expression of Freedom Is in Challenges,
Silence is the price to survive,
Keeping control of the game is false economy,
Debt expansions are hailed,
Answers spread between hiding places,
Someone walks through the garden and looks for tulips,
Some dry leaves begin to fall in summer,
Trials in excesses confuse seasons,
Guardians between brothers are neighbours,
Slavery asks where you come from tired,
The origin answers where I go is the enigma,
The direction of games awaiting progress,
In the midst of tears the vision fades
Where bitterness threatens there are storms,
The cure is in letting the habit suffer go,
When embracing exterior images there are lost steps,
Autumn is death to winter's duel,
Where spring is reborn with the young of summer,
Questions are from the wind and the sea takes them,
Joyful feelings flourish from roots,
Deep down lives the power to share,
Sadness speaks with missed happiness,
Between silences the noises are different,
The company embraces the lonely and they smile,
The trapeze behind curtains attracts minds,
What is the blind light and the darkness of light,
Be or seem the strange question of the smoke,
Leading the strange stranger to the extreme,
Where the direction of the spirit awaits.

THE WORSHIP GAME

In direction the pyramid gives mission to life,
Where critical and controlled system centre,
Magically the story will be a great strategy,
Where thought solves without changes,
Fears embedded in wrapped silences,
A sweet criticism manipulation will be the story,
How to get into the perfect soft shower,
A problem terrifies in calm strategies,
Fearful the steps generate a fall,
Between the crisis light of illusions entertains,
The core of the system is a dark bridge,
People controlled for the hunger game,
The hypnosis of intrigues trapped by a virus,
Dreams of glances waiting for joys,
The sacred tortoise just waits and sighs,
Religions sleep science is language,
Between hello and goodbye the town is still asleep,
A sinister nightmare enters the light and the dark,
The division of a bullet will leave no sounds,
Under the laws of the game there are no chosen screams,
A circle covers the fire of the forbidden mystery,
In the last hour there are rituals under numbers,
Between lightning and thunder the opinions collapse,
Under a game without colours the soul is struck,
The hidden thing is to believe in presence attention,
Under a mysterious sea of lost stars,
The expressions are alignment and dominoes,
Where the rhythm is lost and darkness is born,
With reality of secrets they wrap codes.

HUMAN SLAVE

The quantum leap opens between bushes,
Underground lines lift the tracks,
The sharp claws with a skin green hue,
A force field envelops scales,
The caves wait to take a flight,
Among the search for brothers of the hidden,
Secrets sleep the waters await,
The interest of silence are ancient races,
The stellar gods of the interior,
Vertical falls tell history and life,
The breath opens without union to the united,
A world apart images are raised,
The direction goes up in an armorer carriage,
Under a cloak sheep listen to the shepherd,
Networks catch the majority in the process,
The beliefs of ignorance smile and cry,
Between squares the lambs are separated,
The wolf disappeared because they closed steps,
A caretaker dog only plays with his instincts,
The search for the retreat will be late in abysses,
Every movement is a separation,
The order of time adapts the soft game,
A substance rises without internal values,
The network of neurones is obtained in alignment,
Interior insects with intra-terrain gate,
For food hidden in survival,
The moment of the game in the hands of others,
The expressions are alignment and dominoes,
Consciousness is the way of reconstruction.

THE BEGINNING OF THE KINGDOM

Interplanetary principle for terrestrial blindness,
Pleiad messengers receive memories,
Calls from the low are made prophecies,
Times acclaimed by the third company,
The great dictator time is a leap into darkness,
The capsule is ready for the butcher's arrival,
A gleam of swords drag the judgments,
The earth cracks new pests are heard,
The volcanoes swell their veins burning,
Justice cuts wings with a kiss on the hand,
The symbol is fulfilled without ceasing to see the sky,
A great eclipse comes between the light,
An avalanche reveals itself in dark times,
Under projectiles the nuclear will put the command,
Men consumed no longer protected,
Some leaders are in disappearance,
The lie is the daily routine of the sad world,
A traitor among the peace will light the detonator,
In the guise of a teacher it will not save conflicts,
In all worship there is a war Without harmony,
A rebellion at the return of the end I remember,
Under dying pity repression is born,
The nurturing of power is mind control,
Shelter is offered by polluting the earth,
Wounds open in paths of poverty,
In new dynasties the universe will return,
The new humanity will be born again,
Knowledge grows with sorrows rises,
The resurgent light will leave new changes.

GALACTIC FEDERATION

The indefinite time in doubt without defensive,
Between threats and escapes he seeks refuge,
The human is the only animal in needs,
Under laws and masters hold their nights and days,
Chewing tears in disappointment catches measures,
Rowing images in the hidden stock,
The speed of light in the fight does not let go,
The blue infinity sits in silences with notes,
The common thing is learning love without injury,
Breathing the sun gives itself on a lunar journey,
Courage is surrender to reason without battles,
An underworld falls powerlessly to the fight,
Riding footsteps awaken restlessness,
The desert intoxicates souls in torments,
Where the riding fire does not forget sparks,
In serenity passion softens with veils,
Constancy is the value of the whole seed,
Through the eyes the truth brings smiles,
As the thunder waits before hearing its war,
By revitalising winds with cool night,
The spirit of the air where it does not die even to the ice,
Like a sphere renews the image of mind,
Facing challenges after storms,
The company gathers the changes in roads,
In cordial gestures there are currents of the sea,
With the heart of trust and united affection,
In energy it transforms and rejuvenates,
Mending feelings beyond the eternal,
In balance we are all one at the same time.

THE MAGNETIC FIELDS

Marine uterus plasma of the earth and life,
The first gestation of biological molecules,
Living beings like antennas between the sky of stars,
Transition in transition in challenging fields.
North and south geometry by eastern recesses,
Static union for bird migration,
Tactical door with symphony in frequencies,
All a flight connected with its harmony,
Heart and heartbeat by the thread of the universe,
Protective mantle with permission of light,
Shield with a filter toning radiation,
A whole cycle between a song with music,
Between belts the particles travel far,
A spectacle they leave their colours in the sky,
The gift of sparkles in the northern lights,
Sun moon and earth in storms are wrapped,
More than other conversations electricity is born,
The unique Schulman frequency musical instrument,
Waves in resonance in simultaneous connection,
All shared between delta and alpha state,
Lightning of words in divine production,
Indoor electricity regulator to adapt,
Peace and calm between waterfalls and mountains,
While uneven deserts hide,
Marine vein currents internal cable crossovers,
Nature is the spirit of life treatment,
Temples from the infinite module to the beat,
All alignment is balance of energies,
Where tomorrow and today there wisdom.

THE SEARCH FOR THE SOUL

The masses in dominion by a disguised order,
Tied hand and foot a dagger pierces the mind,
As crosses mark cattle in slaughterhouses,
The paralysis of fear responds with a muzzle to fraud,
In food, advertising is a hidden war,
A driver wakes up when memories arrive,
The ancient of times seeks free paths,
While the cage opens the bars but no one comes out,
Where a path is free without knowing about it,
In hope hatred will open with calm,
Where the marrow is the inner fiver of the spirit,
Suffering is necessary until a time,
Suffering stabilises what you no longer need,
The cultivation of the process renews inner strength,
Where stained past was sunk in delay,
A balance is born after being eaten,
Birth is the key to changing an ending,
An interior speaks for the truth it faces,
Where a mighty earthquake connects the search,
The work of the plan survives in darkness,
Recognising yourself is a wise conversation,
The physicist is a hero to hear changes,
A frequency without sounds reaches the heart,
With the certainty reason drags logic,
A seal of the most chained in the sand,
When you admire the silence you understand the words,
The return is the transformation of the past,
Intuition will be the impulse of the universe,
By connection of the soul in search of harmony.

GUIDELINES FOR HUMANITY

Each song is different invisible in the end,
Like a dance in life some are caught,
As long as he who wants to be first will be last,
A volunteer experiment is to feel constant,
Consciousness makes the construction of the rhythm,
Waking up on earth is like coming out of the dark,
Beliefs believe and wait for the sleeping soul,
The design was the trap to plunge into the deep,
The laws experience everything that goes up comes down,
As time is a slave in the hands of the clock,
Hidden rules empower the opposite,
Among the deaf in a hurry you can't see the signs,
Self-confidence is smart inside,
Shouts of acclaim awaken on earth,
Damaging DNA is blocking the higher self,
The change of separation searches far away,
An embrace of the infinite is united in close proximity,
The frequency system restores DNA,
A new plan synchronises to awaken respect,
The guides show symphonies with impulses,
Traces are set on fire questions,
A cloud of cosmic experiences is born,
Between trust the price of heaven rises,
The next separate search will be sped up,
With self-destruction of trust in leaders,
For the union without having critical fears,
An end of the old energy is the beginning of the new,
For a generation wise in creative harmony,
A high frequency is an instant of love.

THE FIFTH OPEN DIMENSION

The transition will be unstoppable the change an impulse,
Very scared dark elites among bushes,
The high vibration is opening souls,
Hidden leaders plan the fight against,
Attacks against communication are reborn,
Strategies invade the cacti feel,
Accusing the system with crime and insanity,
Quantum leap has already occurred in nature,
In the beginning there are witnesses between years of experiences,
By continuing in the process, suffering is inevitable,
Lie and selfishness will be dense and dark,
Among hunger people will die like wild beasts,
There are entities whose food is the negative,
Not believing is good, resonance is the answer,
The responsibility is not to feed the leader,
An antidote to survival is loving yourself,
The human is generator when using his polarity,
Frequency alignment exists for millennia,
By connecting with the spirit you save envy,
Eliminating suffering generates calming sadness,
Embracing animals is like embracing life,
Song and dance is a healing receptor,
Exercise is waves that release the body,
Loving respect is the greatest repellent to the enemy,
The unstoppable effort will be powerful on the road,
A magic circle will protect the surroundings,
The silence will be able to hear the cries of freedom,
A parallel universe is an active device,
The change would arise in the matter of energies.

CLOSURE OF THE THIRD DIMENSION

Black and white photographs with coloured memories,
Peace will be reborn in the destruction of ashes,
The path is not violence, it is education,
Between some and others there will be cold traces,
Feeling the earth ignites contact in history,
Love is an art of discipline with magic,
Concentration is the practice of overcoming,
You will not be the same when exchanging haste for patience,
The melancholy of the past is quietly forgotten,
There are tears that are necessary to cleanse the pain,
For an incredible life the attraction is the feeling,
By trusting instinct, the experience is different,
Wisdom is loving each other from January to December,
Where the present is lived before the future,
The universe understands no spoken languages,
The frequency is answer with wonders or sorrows,
As infinite freshness is the birth of a rose,
The hug to a tree is the divine vibration,
The signs from heaven are marvellous mirrors,
The guilty will end, the wounds will heal,
The fire will calm the cold when extinguishing the dominions,
Paradises without disguises will swim in clean waters,
Like unicorns and fairies dance in the rain,
Enjoying solitude is knowing yourself,
A thousand dreams are reality the power is the sun and the moon,
While smiles shine talking to the plants,
The heart rejoices between a beat of kisses,
Without time in limitations new seeds will be born,
As we come with nothing the farewell is reciprocal.

THE CALL OF CREATION

The return to the light is the source of courage,
Faith is wisdom with love for life,
Shaking off old beliefs will reconsider minds,
Correction is a collective spiral work,
The stones will feel the wind blow soft,
The power of darkness will be an illusion,
Dimensions bring warriors of light,
Freedom through the truth will be born peace,
Attention will be called for the Resurrection,
An authority will sail without a ship's captain,
The provisional will only be observed on the flight,
Flags of surrender will calmly rise,
A change of command will sound between bubbles,
Where control is the secret already forgotten,
Some things stop others will no longer be seen,
Something visible and transparent recognises pity,
A change seems confusing between free steps,
The dawn of the new will erase the everyday,
Between revelations there are white hats,
The power of control ends with the final breath,
Sounds will filter facts explaining love,
A cleansing of minds calls for calm and harmony,
Desires will live in emotions of progress,
In joyous developments there will be celebrations,
Experience is transparent transformation,
Growth will be a breeze without judging the environment,
Teachers will bring easy ways,
Like a star is admired for its brilliance,
An explosion of the earth will be reborn in life.

THE ODYSSEY SHIELD

Behind the sun a spiritual plane is physical,
Representative constellation stars,
Obedience is of the system always hungry,
In attraction of attention they eat each other,
The dictator is dual united with the beast and the angel,
Followers with hallucinations are sought out,
The interior is thirsty wants freedom and defence,
The struggle with the outside is for power,
Polar structures lose particles due to effects,
The crowd is unity like an anthill,
The aura between spaces has a volume,
The energies communicate telepathically,
The general field is phantom consciousness,
Happiness could be the goal of worship,
Feeling love is the life full of pleasure,
The correct path does not exist it only appears,
Not lowering the shield is a training,
The soul is a mortal door to the immortal,
The reins of life have no other owner,
Protecting feelings enhances personality,
A challenging game is like fire
The cultural value is moral of the emotional reflection,
When living with doubts the energies devour you,
Pride is cornered in the invisible corner,
Everything is duplicated fractal mind and spirit,
Sustained truth lives as an inner teacher,
Between ties of imagination powers are born,
The source of the force need not be armed,
The spell of control is in consciousness.

EXECUTE HUMANITY

The company between escapes does not cling to others,
Where the population believes in protection,
The origin finds a way to gently reduce,
When creating the problem the solution is already acted upon,
Instrument to execute is to use the plan to take care,
Wild beasts support euthanasia in hospitals,
A routine will be an imposition for bad news,
To terrify the weak is to win prisons without surveillance,
Some must be obedient instruments,
The unnecessary part is expensive for the economy,
Start with old age which does not produce is the objective,
The society between corners will be selected,
The creaking of the heart and reason are forgotten,
The sentence (I can't) will be tense and shared,
Many sleepers will go alone to the slaughterhouse,
Planned treatments act on the mind,
Emotional crisis will be real in the face of fear,
The stupid will believe it all and kneel down,
They will beg for salvation from the leader who rejoices,
They disguise compassion in safe vaccination,
They will bathe in love in tears of blood,
Chills on the ground will spill pain,
Due to lack of training, battles are lost,
The human machine will stop deteriorating,
A new generation stage must be born,
Gradually a small population rises,
People will organise peace camps,
Counsellors will try in flames to save humans,
Guides will try to exchange hate for love.

PLANT YOUR OWN TREE

A doll that does not exist will become a myth,
The invasion of the dark force will fall asleep,
The eye of the pyramid will suffer in rebellion,
The dialectical mixture will be waiting for the return,
The foundation orchestra has no challenges,
The battle of heaven will fall from a pendulum,
Dying or living these are the new or old clothes,
The new looks will open secrets on heights,
Love is the law that sustains the universe,
Sweet-hearted humans are in gestation,
The sacredness of life is in the valleys and lagoons,
In the universal the source starts from the one,
The answer of the truth is in the logic,
There are no wonders saved only shared,
The coward for fear will die in his spirit,
Nightmares must purify the soul,
To save experiences in peace is to advance searches,
Forgiveness is enlightenment of love and harmony,
Learning to live is to forget the submerged mud,
A new man cannot be blindly dominated,
The treasure of secrets will erase elites,
The verb touches the soul when codes are opened,
The seeds of revelation will heal wounds,
A balm of harmony is your own will,
The voice of the heart is to awaken the inner child,
A dance with the sun is to share values,
Where eternal youth will be born in brilliance,
The symphony is the choice of practice,
As every day is one more day of school.

PLANETARY AWAKENING

A game of the matrix with codes of light,
Planet earth ascending under tune,
The speed of perception opens other paths,
Different bloodlines are still the roots,
The unequal shape is the trapped position,
In flat missions they descend into the interior,
Between evolution the process attracts energies,
Matter vibrates through forms and positions,
Dimensional descents mark the awakening,
There are prey of the game without using tools,
The image in the meeting makes the symphony,
In speed is the direction of thought,
The mirror is a channel for the impact sought,
It is hot but the darkness of light is cold,
Between messenger codes the cosmos travels,
Hear the roar of the earth when it trembles,
Where in reviews there are ambiguous searches,
A paradise indicates the unreal of the origin in theory,
Evolution breaks free from capitalism,
Among the force of light is the divine creation,
The reason is the first evolution of the step,
The impulse was the first thought of will,
Where creation was the seed of the intellectual,
The search for the truth is infinite to grow,
All disappointments are caught in measures,
Between two atoms the speed is relative,
Everything observed affects the balance,
The invisible particle is the window of progress,
With elegance of colours it surrounds edges.

THE DREAM IS ALREADY WRITTEN

While you breathe you smile then thank,
Walk quietly enjoy the nature landscape,
Make the way kept an interior silence,
Dive into the eternal journey of yourself,
In need of companionship only hugs the animals,
Don't chase anything or anyone for calming down sorrows,
Make up a concert of sweet songs,
Create sublime images with the scent of roses,
Prepare a symphony that will take you to paradise,
Do not make efforts to ask for something in vain,
Feel what it is for you and it will always find you,
All this dream that you live is already written,
Let only existence make the plan,
The help solution is that you swim in peace,
Let life surprise you just trust yourself,
Embrace your Health every day with an air kiss,
Open your heart to moments of pleasure,
Appreciate the people who give you their time,
Everything is perfect where the environment is respected,
Live like the eagle enjoying your goal,
Never ignore the people who miss you,
Tell the brain not to think too much,
Plant your own tree to have your shade,
Do not condemn anyone, each one wears his cross,
Do not be in competition, each one has his game,
Train your mind to the knowledge you enjoy,
Every time you cry you purify and vent,
Not going back is wisdom not to repeat,
A story ends and a new star rises .

I GIVE YOU ON THIS DAY

In memories time does not exist in the morning,
Your crystalline eyes seek happy glances,
For reason and cause that balance demands,
The reflection of life in learning the word,
I like the clinging company of your silence,
That a chosen song can become a letter,
I like to ask for your hand to rest a while,
When you turn on your smile light nostalgia catches me,
I like to see you in the dark and in the sudden sun,
Your wealth of not asking since thanking is everything,
I like that your being trusts my company,
Feeling better every day with your memory is enough for me,
I like your identity of being happy between sorrows,
What is called problems you say are choices,
I like the eternity kept in your heart,
The constant of choosing where you take a moment,
I like your image that appreciates free nature,
Your attentive present that is not distracted from the past,
I like your fantasy that does not stop in the void,
Your protection of the environment like a bird to its nest,
I fully like to feel your awakening without haste,
Do not entertain the boring ones taught me your wisdom,
I like the secret of your story in your look,
I appreciate knowing about your life what you overcome inside,
Your losses with suffering carry flowers at the top,
You enjoy the white snow without distracting your way,
Tomorrow and now your rhythm notes sound,
Your great fragrance rests in your deep sense,
A caress I send you with this poem in glitter.

MYSTERIOUS MIRROR

Some beautiful dimensions swallow me,
Between them I fall into oblivion of time,
With passion of the higher frequency there is evolution,
A stepping stone in human consciousness in brilliance,
By binding itself in the essence the divine rests,
Cosmic awakening that transcends channeling,
In distant forces they leave traces to the call,
Inter-dimensional beings located in other planes,
From above the transmissions connect,
An original fountain that engenders a garden,
The Arcturians from the northern celestial star,
Where the fifth dimension brings healing emotions,
By opening an energetic portal souls enter,
With the language of the wind for a kingdom of justice,
Circulating regularly on earth to save it,
The alpha centaurs with advancements of technology,
Bringing inspirational ideas to humanity,
The Lyres crossed in lines of descent,
Benevolent help is to intervene to help,
The Pleiades a warned of the grays
With their serene gaze they are guides of orientation,
Vegans bring reminder interventions,
Between galactic events to return to the field,
The Andromeda's with their varied heights,
Divine beauty sparkles between her bluish skin,
Authors in messengers with global light codes,
Between illusion and life there is only one choice.
When meeting in the twilight comes victory,
Wake up from death to the beginning.

MEMORIES FOR HONOUR

A person is worth what he does,
Before promises the laws make burdens,
Our wounds are like broken glass,
By not healing their pieces, others are in danger,
The footprints always go with the united spirit,
In choices, consciousness directs senses,
The moments that come are always correct,
Between doubts dreams are lost,
The gods are slavery to programs,
With the emotions in connection you free yourself,
Obedience blinds the colours of life,
Fly without crawling because crawling is ruin,
A grateful heart is a magnet for miracles,
Courage is knowing that one is perfectly imperfect,
The worst cages are those of fear and appearances,
Seeds are actions waiting for fruits,
Past present future are linear concepts,
The best light is in piercing the darkness itself,
We are infinite in temporary bodies,
As the light surrounds the flame that is the truth,
Good is done in silence the rest is theatre,
Your body gets sick to heal the soul,
Fascism is cured by reading racism traveling,
As in giving thanks more strength is born,
Nothing weighs down the road when loaded with love,
The only impossible thing is what is not tried,
Life does not remove things it only frees loads,
The more you know the interior then less you need,
As the cry of birth is silence when dying.

AKE OFF THE VEIL

New lands are flooded with surviving flowers,
The birds rehearse their majestic songs,
Privileged fertile lands glow in the dark,
The atomised world must wake up to the storm,
Humanity trembles hearing between the fight,
Women without inheritance will fertilise monsters,
The man of tomorrow will be chosen by the semen,
The woman will look for children in selective laboratories,
Athletic and intellectual men will be reserve,
Crystalline bones will be disasters in genes,
Between some hands strategies are paralysed,
Mysterious rays invisible to electronics,
Artificial kites will dominate hatred for unions,
The invaded seas will lack immense algae,
Flying on the heights beings from other planets,
Angels of the old appear to erase the bad,
Yesterday's mass will be Protestant without being it,
The world will go searching without seeing it will fall and rise,
Mystical interplanetary es try to impose faith,
Science will deny aliens then it will doubt it,
For centuries they watch over us and entities watch us,
After a final artificial blood will be mechanism,
As it is a privilege to be a candle in the dark,
The interior of the earth will be discovered from oblivion,
Only in moments does civilisation begin to adapt,
The lunar crater will reveal secrets of the seven steps,
A blind world will fall into its vicious ravages,
Suffering and happiness is mathematics of the chosen result,
The artificial doll will devour the creator.

INFILTRATED

Warriors of light enter captive waves,
Existence sequestered by eternal matter of eons,
Groups of aliens with dark forces,
Rules of the new order in abduction and interventions,
Reincarnation observed for experiments,
Androids with compliant program intent,
Burrows with interests looking for servant races,
Reproductive seeds with DNA tests,
Memory suppression is common in processes,
Constant domain for experimental genetics,
Concentration camps for underground food,
Cloning attempts between animals and humanity,
Endings with strategies for mental manipulation,
Memory banks by computer and neural network,
In a sleeping city an umbrella shelters,
Human reptilians the grey workers caste,
Visual and audio spies for looking into hoaxes,
Science studying for the aura humans in matrix,
Recycling of the soul is to force harmony to cruelty,
Projects created under nuclear disguises,
Hall of nightmares in underground laboratories,
Astral travel with manipulation in matter,
Embryonic cloning between human and alien,
Rapid replication of bodies by means of light and energy,
Caged areas for unexpected kidnappings,
Gray telepathy listening to minds around,
In a war of flashes the black triangle is the insignia,
Under tunnels of power the category is not altered,
The system game has no middle ground.

A LOST WATCH

An old man is sitting listening to his past,
Whispers approach with questions in step,
Images are transformed that someone comes to hug him,
Smiles surround greetings when commenting on a finding,
A student lighting up his big boy eyes,
The already elderly professor on the bench hears his phrase,
The young man comments on having collected dignity from his legacy,
The elderly teacher asks some teaching,
What anecdote was most appreciated in the childhood of the class,
The young man tells the story when he was a student,
A colleague shows a watch that I liked,
With exploits in envy of his pocket I have stolen it,
Complaints arrive instantly for claiming what was lost,
Silence everyone in class accused of a crime,
The teacher with patience in the wise solving,
Nobody leaves the class without going to be checked,
Students without problems leave their hands free,
The professor proposes calmly, he will look for all pockets,
Proposing every child to keep their eyes closed,
The serene professor finds the trapped watch,
A whole silence turns on and the clock was returned,
Curiously, nobody calls the young man accused,
In professor declares the search with closed eyes,
In order not to accuse a wrong child for a bad act,
The child so shocked with happiness appreciates it,
The young man already graduated was inspired to heal instincts,
The teacher teaches understood, an error has a way out,
A second is the cause, the third is a crack,
By educating by example, one perceives what life is.

SENTIMENTAL ENCOUNTER

A firefly shines in the dark sweet night,
In the distance some shadows hide,
Some with memories of fiery experiences,
Flames of the past are enveloped dreamer,
Shines with beautiful images leave silent footsteps,
They look for love in nostalgia like a lost refuge,
In the distance they feel a loss waiting,
They unite with memories nature that forms horizons,
There are no angry noises only lost smiles,
Like a phantom questions fade away,
A few sighs escape with the smell of strawberries and flowers,
Falling into the wheat water between snowy and hot.
The looks are confused for getting lost in the north,
On the shore sleeping a dove looks out,
Between night and tomorrow falling stars fell,
A dew on the top blew wind on the branches,
Ashes were wrong to be alone in the flames,
In dust will remain words with traces of love,
Some empty songs ran through the landscapes,
Some hugs in ivory verses are sealed,
Among invisible roses the wounds remained,
A few kisses of butterflies chased each other and fled,
The imprisoned lips felt provocation in delusions,
On the bare sand is the golden sun between clouds,
Luminous joyful encounter that remains in oblivion,
Fugitive from sadness in transparent melancholy,
Some storks take the adventures of time,
The wind sounds in regrets, just blow out the candle,
Because wanting through cracks is early morning in sorrows.

A GHOST PARK

With illusions he marked his destiny and he never wanted to escape,
Him let the sky turn grey and it never came back
The ghost park wraps cement in corners,
Between turns laughter is heard loud for attention,
Mindless images rush through material,
A monster without memories is constantly hungry,
Some falls with sorrows choose addicted herbs,
Over internal silences a few drinks provide oblivion,
There are iron windows that are game endings,
Some cries of sorrows await missed visits,
Memories of the past suddenly appear,
Friends are becoming blind eyes of the moment,
Family members are the roots to embrace wounds,
In desperate crosses memory arrives in order,
The signals stop taking the quiet course,
The catch is in the cruise when you repeat getting on,
The clock points with arrows the environment is trapped,
The days and nights face without waiting for the damaged,
The sky changes colours to attract the glances,
A kiss can be lost aimlessly in the mornings,
When picking up their sorrows is only to mourn them,
Letting go is the simple thing to go in search of it brings more sorrow,
Sadness is inevitable but suffering it is optional,
Letting go of those who do not love you is loving what you are,
Pain is in oneself if a foot leaves you at your destination,
The outside comes and goes, the company is oneself,
The sea rises to the sky and goes down the mountains free,
From animals you learn their love is our guide,
The secret park says you are your faithful recreational.

SINGLE MOON LIGHT (LENNON)

Between everything and nothing shines silence and calm,
Embracing destiny with singing sunsets,
Peaceful is the window open to gardens,
A romantic look is wrapped in colours,
Towards tomorrow and today there is no real time,
The bohemian nights dipped in stars,
There are paths with flowers in eternal romances,
I want to understand the search for the love of verses,
In enchanted forests only silences attract,
Trapped in childhood my interior is wrapped,
Between empty walls writings free me,
Lonely escapes hurt my happy eyes,
Where the environment hinders peace with noise,
Intrigues carry the years with hidden silences,
I like hiding places so as not to look far,
Success is a cruise where the ship stops,
When you feel the footprints the roots are released,
The sound makes the dream come true without questions,
In the middle of the bridges the soul stops,
The dreamers in flashes feel calls,
The passage of the dream comes from the sincere heart,
Among the lights of applause there are indomitable,
Passing around corners only involves fears,
The games appear seeds without giving flowers,
A special story lifts a druid veil,
The separation of magic controls the order,
Where there is a small environment I imagine someone,
Between dreams fade the last hours,
In the search I wake up and in it I fell asleep.

A WOUNDED CUP (AMY. W.H)

In the physical world I feel separate bubbles,
Divided spheres are raining on wet,
I am confused by experience with illusion,
I can't find the value of the hidden game's,
There are surfaces with levels survival,
In each layer can be feel smiles or sadness,
I want to be a plant with easy metamorphosis,
I hate umbilical cord frequencies,
The field of the paranormal numbs me,
While the hypnotic trigger is activated,
Disobedience is my code of happiness,
Between the tears my makeup falls asleep,
Under silences of love my soul hides,
Dark colours surround me with magic
With my eyes I look for miracles of Freedom,
Arrows flood my disobedient heart,
Where I get drunk with addicted calm,
In a bright bar I deceive my thoughts,
Feelings hurt between cup sounds,
There are doors with keys and between silent screams,
Sunsets inspire me to write about you,
I see you and I don't know you,
I feel you and I don't have you,
The nights are like an empty black hole,
In days I just look at the ground I'm tired
Some trees take me to the highest peak,
Through the slits there are jazz trumpets blowing,
Some sad pages leave footprints with flowers,
As long as he squeezes my heart into lies,
Peaceful obedience comes and makes me sleepy.

FIRE STAR (E. PRESLEY)

A heart open to inevitable success is born,
A book from the moon to reach the stars,
Where a root of cells rises to falls,
Child's face envelops heart of burning sun,
In bursts of success his immense colour of voice,
Compete for trophies in a fast-paced jungle,
Among suspicious rules, exits are chosen,
A wise man owns my mind unhurriedly tells me,
I don't believe in anything I see everything Its suspicious,
Rushing is inevitable I'm in love,
I must not stay it is a sin to be able to hurt,
When I take her hand to mine the emptiness disappears,
With a safe mind I go face to love,
Defying the danger between kisses and pleasures,
With beautiful moments in forbidden games,
Bridging inexplicable emotional differences,
In the sentimental unleashing empty pleasures,
Discovering deliveries my soul narrows,
In a stone of love I embrace myself for purposes,
Desiring tenderness eternal follies are unleashed,
With my back to the world I feel like being an owner,
I go blind down the street separating love,
At the end of the trial I can't find her kisses,
The colour of honey mixes with no sweet taste,
Exterior light turned off for living in the bodies,
The forgetfulness of the inner light hides tears,
The shared history remains in footprints,
In a sphere without forgetfulness the first King was born,
Without tears songs of goodbye are wrapped.

THREE BIRDS (B. MARLEY)

Flights in shadows with eagle wings,
Free steps between some with ties,
Hopes in the mountains of the world,
Streets with breezes open fire of success,
Without fear my soul lives calmly
The legendary has no skin colour,
Music talent is the magic of births,
On the notes there is a part of me,
In each encounter the mind carries messages,
Where childhood is innocence,
Children should smile says consciousness,
In childhood mirrors are teaching breezes,
Broadcasting a bridge back to life,
Moments of silence are discoveries,
Between the meeting of the value of who you are,
Understanding who values you with feelings,
With sweet smiles energy is appreciated,
The weight of the challenge surprises with loneliness,
When losing beings of peace the spirit only cries,
The sincere environment is rarely crossed,
A home is the way where everything is,
Without coming to submit or to submit to anyone,
Money can't buy eternity,
To be able to conquer interprets to see joys,
The bible is the record of beginnings,
Without negligence, harm or pride,
The best life interpreter is to feel paradise,
The rebellion and revolution try to open slavery,
The roots are sacred my guitar harmonies.

NEVER EVER (M .JACKSON)

With roots trapped in miseries and silences,
Many days passed in childhood they were lost,
The look of my shadow pursues me in pain,
There are cold nights with grey days and no exits,
In the lap of whispers a laugh is heard,
Wrapping an image appears a disguise,
Calm fills the void by putting on a makeup,
Passions fly between happy drawings,
Where a child is reborn playing secretly,
The heart opens with united hopes,
There are loose stars like comets shining,
In the dances of time a child is still asleep,
The invisible thrills me with the crowd enjoyed,
Far distances creep with me near,
In a kindness the answer hides something cold,
Between the internal state the exterior I see it blind,
Separating boundaries in chosen adventures,
Doing strange sorrows in faces of joy,
Monsters appear that force me to submit,
New world swallows me stuck to a secret,
My soul runs in the wind without finding a way out,
There is no going back the game already caught me,
The memories are still young in an adult being,
The unforgettable heart desires an interpreter,
Where souls with screams their voices cheer him,
I seek a friend in the mirror that reflects sincerely,
The tears are dry with different eyes
Erase the terror of fear to feel again,
Healing the world is a message from the sleeping king.

IS ANYBODY THERE.(QUEEN)

I have a beautiful dream to tell to the moon,
In a crystal cave butterflies awaken,
Some defeated are mixed between colours,
Some lost and sad fears hide,
I feel like a caged genie with restraints,
I don't feel safe because murmurs hurt,
There are nomadic moments with sleeping beauty,
Some surrender caresses seem lost,
Somewhere in the universe they will leave traces,
I don't want to wake up the day gets dark,
An intern space trembles over a poem,
The crowd terrifies me with an empty inside,
Where is the breeze and where the exit is hidden,
Continuing with success leads to my happiness,
The forces of destiny offer me company,
Where the immensity is submerged in sadness,
Voice of the soul sings bitter lines of time,
Tears are wrapped in soft company,
The search for silences lost in no place,
To go ahead is to fly between dimensions,
Bells will always leave my name,
Between sweet memories there is a beautiful breath,
Some voices deliver the rhythms of births,
From heaven all good shouts celebration
The celestial of looks recovers eternal life,
I will always be a seagull in the immense beautiful sea,
The delusions of the cold and free air are irresistible,
The encounter of heat will only be born when I die,
Between the fairy books my self will continue to smile.

THE TUNNEL OF LIFE

A space that descends to the sea of life,
With dimensions beyond the physical,
A fetus enters the body opening joys,
Wind chimes listening to the welcome,
There are no gaps in the keys to progress,
The creation of the atmosphere is hope's,
A belly is the immense is paradise and it's remembered,
Among comfortable sounds is the love base,
The stars are surrounded by mountains,
Where there are emotions in the family of seas,
The tunnel passage is a small bridge,
An equilibrium point is activated in energies,
Some perspectives of emotions are learning,
In feelings with sweetness there is no exits end.
A teddy bear sends kisses from the sky,
From space births send signals,
The music is soft with beautiful dimensions,
Between small words seconds are unforgettable,
Like a good guest his arrival is lights,
His departure is the same by smiles traces,
Some photos in the rain speak of the sun,
There are short encounters but eternal fantasies,
Fleeting memories are unexpected light
Spring breeze keeps options open,
If Starry nights seek only diamonds,
In the blind search few manage to polish themselves,
Setting a wise example is nurturing harmony,
There is no return to change a past,
But if there is a beginning to love the end.

THE CHANGE OF DNA

The ancient times asleep and altered,
Between movements the paths are modified,
For hidden separations there are armies,
Believers are approaching long changes,
Apocalypse terms descend from heaven,
The times bring reflections with reflections,
Returning to the seas with enigmas,
Plans of secrets evolving in silence,
Since then in centuries there are reptiles,
Dragon peoples in violence and distances,
From the sky enter the grey traveler,
Between vaccines some prey will be the origin,
A colossal plague will come in check and caution,
The game of chance reaches the end of rules,
Where an encounter is whipping elections,
Earthquakes without borders will not be able to cure penalties,
Disappointments will open from the deserts,
It will awaken the internal fire of the earth,
The last performances will be history,
The red bridge will go to suffering,
The city raises its arms faints in fear,
An eagle's flight will turn into a raven,
In fierce falling waters gush forth in lightning,
Doors will be closed with protected trips,
Radiations lose the air like galaxies,
The mental file came to delusions of the world,
It is the fourth dimension for mystery science,
They are among us for holograms,
There is no turning back the night came with the day.

THE PERFECT CHESS

The work of art does not ask questions of the creator,
A tournament Wrapped between battles without cheating,
Between the defence checkmate doubles steps,
In a capture a bishop enters threats,
From anaesthetised pawns they look captured,
A lady in control takes her instincts wise,
A galloping horse closes chains thinking,
A movement is born with tricks and measures,
Between brave opportunistic towers are wrapped,
The protection of the environment has keys,
A frost is felt by opponents and falls,
Reconquests and advantages in deep senses,
On each side conditions were shaking,
An isolation is wrapped in looks,
Something invisible is reinforced with antidotes,
Where a look is born aggressive and spicy,
Ingenious minds don't capture the great outdoors,
Sighs with firm controls are raised,
Maintaining companionship is paramount,
Rapid part development is delivery,
The moment is the magic in taking direction,
Miserable punishments lose harmony,
Among advantages there are suffering without exits,
An eternal calm is defined as a hero,
Time of threats and flight seek refuge,
Capturing the royal crown by sacrifice,
Without haste the attention is to catch the rivals,
The tournament in the life hacks is a second,
With the triumph for the value of the infinite king.

THE HAPPY GREY-EYED PARROT

One day I passed by your side and I saw your smile shining,
Your big gray eyes with splendour were getting closer,
Your look was anxious looking for intrigue,
An intense kiss told funny stories,
When I gave you a greeting you gave me a bite,
Between silences I listening to your phrases,
Some colours made the mixtures of the soul,
Between jumps of joys your environment is enveloped,
Surrounding your interior a mystery tells me,
The landscapes are green and I like my house,
The shining sun brought the scent of flowers,
Like a poppy seed I feel the roots,
Hearts of treasure feed my days,
In a raft of infinity i built the whole,
To collect memories and never forget them,
The mission of life with the most sincere love,
Filling hearts with wise glitters,
Understanding that my step was more than company,
In discouragement my presence lifted spirits,
Where there are shadows I illuminate with my soft plumage,
Whenever you turn to the side you'll see me come back,
In every corner of the house my presence follows,
Between light and darkness is my air,
The greetings will be eternal when entering or leaving,
Between emotions is the breeze with pure love,
Beyond like an angel there will be unions,
From the dimensions in trust I have lived,
With dignity I dismiss the delivery said healthy,
Between verses my happy union remains.

THE CANDLE AND THE MATCH

A close rendezvous peeked out in intrigue,
Among a mysterious sound a spark was heard,
To say that life is a temporary step,
Just a second is worth more than time,
In a cave to be spiritual is to be aware,
On a certain day the eyes met,
The questions stand out amid hidden fears,
A telepathic conversation with doubts is born,
Said the candle of fear if the match lights,
As you approach my side the days are numbered,
Deliveries brush glances with the flame out,
The match just waits on a cold comment,
I only count seconds to turn on without a path,
In waiting fantasies dreams fade,
The dream mission is the vivid experience,
Between the waiting candle the evenings do not sigh,
Emotions of the soul are jewels only lit,
As the match approached the candle gave smiles,
Between the glow on sensations are born,
Some notes are wrapped in pain and joys,
Some smoke and songs pass through the cracks,
There is a wind that envelops cold heat and laughter,
The experience of life only between two is activated,
As caresses speak when joining in smiles,
I don't want them to shut up when they leave joy,
Putting your hand in mine are like stars to the sky,
As the gaze travels in the infinite mystery,
Scorching fire is like frozen ice,
So yesterday won't be tomorrow,
In hugging memories.

THE PORTAL OF THE MIND

To love is to vibrate in Freedom of the environment,
Suffering is a companion of the ego,
Among the confusing is the need for attachment,
The self is light in the dark,
Nothing and nobody belongs to us, the only thing is being,
When enjoying a dessert you forget the rush,
The best gift is to think about smiling,
Remember that every day more is a day less,
Make happy is the eternal union of the interior,
As the raindrops fall on the perfect,
Distance is the test of the truth told,
The heart feels the head understands tomorrow,
Even if you remove your footprints they always remain,
Any damage has the cure from love,
Without fear in works waiting fountains flow,
The moments are the keys to the challenge,
Desires are the roots of eternal progress,
One chance is given the second is won,
The truth waits only the lie is in a hurry,
Whoever misses you looks for you still in lost battles,
No one is better or worse comparison is wasting time,
Real love comes without asking how to sleep without doubting,
Wisdom without begging solves lost intelligence,
Trusting waiting answers miracles,
The attitude does not change, only lose battles that you leave,
From enigmas good processes raise works,
This is how the soul reflects a slender and strong jaguar,
Like an embrace of light without stones on the way,
Heals the entire land of shadows and darkness.

THE COVENANT OF SECRET

An illusion which escapes in perceptions,
Where the most awake will be accused insane,
In the objectives there are no visible suspects,
An expanded knowledge is in danger of death,
Weaken minds are the roots of the project,
Accelerator metals to age fast,
The method of control from transgenic foods,
A rebellion will be the mild poison of the environment,
Fear will be the weapon of any opposition,
Separation is religion and politics,
Under soft comments the agreements are key,
Entertaining with hates feelings will divide,
Where games with slaughter are raising the blind,
With images and sounds tools are daggers,
The truth will be accompanied by believing in protection,
Vaccines will be required to track crime,
The title of the majority will be unarmed insects,
In intentional recruits minorities are chosen,
The secret of the truth will be awarded in titles,
The prizes for good steps will be cheats,
With crimes for disagreements for the slave base,
The truth will hide sadness in their faces,
A prison of self-deception will be dominant,
In distraction the autopilot goes off,
A field around is only a puppet of the user,
The covenant of secrecy will be the fury of unions,
When feeling inside it would be an enemy weapon,
Where the secret would fall in the dark.

CONQUER THE UNIVERSE

Threat of climate change opens distant ideals,
Some immense stars attract exterior that observes,
Explorations approaching the Galactic Odyssey,
Each planetary system will have pole attraction,
Between ice and storms the waves will be varied,
The Gods of Olympus will attract ships with telepathy,
The universe is an atlas with traveler calls,
The propellant photons awaken other entities,
Guides will be sent from shining stars
The beats must be united in solidarity groups,
Between keys and mysteries the meteorites are frontiers,
Some giants move the universe is their home,
Between comets and laxer challenges they find becoming,
Some planets haunt emotions for control
Unknown forces trap the thoughts,
Some entities feed on the energies of others,
In electrical matter the weak are at risk,
Wrapping calm in appearances they look for fluids,
Bodies is the target to reserve food,
The enigmas of the universe have several shelters,
Some absorb knowledge to enslave,
Zombies can be created by dark forces,
The universe is ambition to be variety of the whole,
In some waterfalls there is spell protection,
The transformations are like mutant plants,
Between energies the secrets will have a goal,
In the magical and mysterious the great lady wraps herself,
It is the moon of memories with the solar eclipse wrapped,
Where nothingness and everything eliminated the clock of time.

THE ROOT OF PROBLEMS

Visions linked to reality detect the ego,
The domination of opinion and decision between the sword,
Controversial control in constant movements,
A power seized with masked identity,
By absorbing the energy it tries to annihilate the heart,
The steps without freeing themselves hide false fortresses,
His arrogance thwarts by believing in conflicts,
Clarity makes us visible by activating instinct,
A war is not a good way to protect the calm,
Illuminating in consciousness one transcends to the top,
The past is studied with harmony of understanding,
A powerful voice that becomes a tool,
An impulse that wraps claws to get to control,
The target is detected to put an end to advance,
A centre carries traces of emotions and thoughts,
The most recognised opinion makes you feel superior,
It is the chain of the ego that separates universal love,
Conditions arrogantly lose pleasure in living,
There are foods that society instills in obedience,
Memories of the past integrate the ego to put you to sleep,
The I am is the attachment of beliefs to put a price,
Wanting to compete is a danger to blind satisfaction,
Uncontrollable desire buys more than it needs,
Obsession for outward appearance swallows the spirit,
In despair, life is lost for worrying,
Imitations block the natural phases of life,
Diseases are addicted by continuous cheating,
Recordings mark birth and human development,
The ancient being must die to be reborn from its ashes.

MICROCHIPS

From freedom to slave is the destiny cocktail,
The wicked pact is already in active condition,
Illicit trafficking leads to ethnic cleansing,
The interference scars are raised,
Extractions like implants are firm targets,
Brain control by means of antenna micro wires,
In a laboratory they pursue success to catch fears,
Towards eager races the heights are headed,
Demanding shadows keep private chains,
Members chase faces that smile obediently,
The rules of the trip put the issue of monetary security,
Laws of the system develop fanciful hiding places,
The puppets participate in the historical game,
The unconscious kindles flames to the hidden feeling,
Exuberant words transform so as not to discover themselves,
To restore imagination of enigmas is to work together,
Awakening evolves sources with great privileges,
A stable future awaits the thief to be locked up,
The game is like a puzzle you must complete the story,
Nano technology integrated into the microscopic bacteria,
Where integration will converse with DNA,
The harmony in his features only silences the traces,
Particles explore electronics in ideas,
All matter is convertible into a wave from beyond,
A new knowledge arrives to continue exploring,
The difference between the sun the scale will be magnetic,
The infinite car in dimension and constant movement,
The alphabet of chemistry combined in molecules,
Knowing who you are not screams awakening from the dream.

THE MAGIC SHOP

When entering a store someone offered wonders,
When asking, I'm looking for a gift for my birthday,
Answered here all are the most precious,
Some beautiful bottles written with a message,
Contemplating written vases were friendly hands,
One shoe recording with an effort is started,
Some drew flowers, other song notes,
The choice was simple with the possibility accepted,
They had no definitive price only a sign was shining,
The price of purchases was optional of the customer,
Some colourful packages wrote a few words,
With very elegant signs they offered their hugs,
Some written glass said I am wisdom,
Other boxes with music named hope's,,
Some boats of secrets shine with courage,
Some cartons of poems sold the tranquility,
A small sphere had fruits with emotions,
In a small corner a doll said happiness,
A drawn jasmine talked about giving is not commented,
Some dry leaves turn the image into canvases,
Bitter lemons say their flavour balances,
Says the sun with the moon intuition is a star,
A circle marks a labyrinth to know exits,
A few drops of rain refresh love with fantasies,
A ticket signs a stamp so as not to forget the roots,
A nail says brothers are like fingers of the hand,
Some seeds indicate that the beginning is to plant oneself,
The water by a source account of the feeling is born,
Where the endless meets the spirit with the soul.

IRREVERSIBLE CODE

What you carry in your pocket does not make you admirable,
What you carry in your heart makes you admirable,
Beginnings are progress to dance with stars,
Since ancient times it is advanced by abundance,
The excuse is a reason to relate a purpose,
Inside the instinct real life is reproduced,
When you know yourself you become powerful,
When you accept yourself you become invincible,
Books cure ignorance to understand inequality,
Love is leaving your head to enter your heart,
Think less and feel more to build confidence,
What is for you, even if you take off, will haunt you,
What is not for you even if you insist will disappear,
Each person on his way chooses what he needs the most,
Each person in his path is the value of what he offers,
You are like the magnet, everything you feel and think attracts,
The value of essence is invisible when searching in need,
Loving yourself is the courage not to hurt others,
When you refuse to look at yourself, life puts foreign mirrors on you,
To find what you are looking for be happy with what you have,
He who is a friend of all is not a friend of anyone,
The outer beauty does not define the inside of the treasure,
As what shines is not gold, the rusty dies,
The flavours have their defined identity to choose from,
As reason has setbacks with the heart,
The mixtures found must be compatible,
Civilisation is destined like Atlantis,
A brave man decided to burn himself in the fire of the dragon,
And that was not the end, it was the beginning of a story.

MISTAKES

All relationships are teachers who have learnings,
You must be wrong to know that this is not failure,
You must blame others to know that they are free,
You must look inside since the others are mirrors,
You must fall to know what it costs to get up,
You must stay alone to appreciate that it is company,
You must cry to know what a blessing it is to be happy,
You must disappear to know what it is to find yourself,
You must fall out of love to know that love is you,
You must stumble to observe the steps,
You must be cold to know how to share a coat,
You must go hungry to know how to offer food,
You must feel the words to know what they hurt,
You must fall into the traps to avoid more holes,
You must feel the pain to appreciate the sick,
You must feel angry to know how to appreciate calm,
You must feel the noise to appreciate the peace of silence,
You must feel a fall to be aware of the road,
You should always try to know that if you can,
You must have conflicts to know how to ignore them,
You must take a hit to feel like not sharing it
You must feel the war to seek harmony,
You must lose a loved one to know how to comfort,
You must feel the abandonment to know how to give appreciation,
You must be sick to feel what health is,
You must take care of the thoughts because they are destiny,
You must stop rubbing the lamp because you are the genie,
You must know that growing is sharing, not competing,
We get wiser with setbacks, not with time .

A THOUSAND YEARS SLEEPING

The woman is a portal, the man is the key,
In the strangeness of time, nothing awaits and heals pain,
Some storks are caught in a dark nightmare,
Where a life is extinguished with pain for demands,
Plants are saddened by continual threats,
Some horses gallop to go in high mountains,
Ships with aliens loom in the skies,
The union becomes visible with invisible uncertainty,
The rivers grunt with stones amid wild currents,
Some birds seek their rhythm due to polar disturbances,
Humans run in haste to save the havoc,
The air is wrapped with traps to follow strategies,
They strike the feelings separating the borders,
Some strong ideas experiment with chemistry,
Different contrary ideas are wrapped in the tracks,
Cryptobiosis is the perfect plan, system and great enigma,
Viruses are in the corner to feel exhausted,
Damage is inevitable only going to sleep saves the earth,
The sturdy woods scream inland for oxygen,
The darkness steals the brilliance of the green spirit reign,
A cry dream repair will be the established law,
The predator looks to the outside to escape,
For continuous days monsters will fall in storms,
All dark matter wraps itself in a spiral galaxy,
History is companion for time in disappearance,
Between small and giants the stars leave traces,
The memories of the universe with the atoms persist,
The mead of the gods leaves the cultural formula,
The woman is reborn to the fetus and the man protects him.

CUSTOM

Ingredients the same dish constantly cooked,
The everyday of life caught in the doubles,
Seekers of purity waiting for contemplation,
Magic reactions for an exhausting spell,
Aspired practices in forgetfulness of the inner principle,
Mantra spells searching for salvations,
The excuses with the fanatic constancy catching,
Impulsive consumers looking for temples of love,
In lighting there are traps if you look for necessities,
The path of ancient patterns can swallow dreams,
When feeling a defeat in the ego, panic appears,
The supreme realm finds the very court of the soul,
Morality in parallel inquires into private property,
Dialogues in the head generating emotional sensation,
The voids are perceived with irritation of conformity,
Laziness is a distraction that comes to oppose,
Between anger and empathy the devil fights the spiritual soul,
Intrigue is the enigma to surrender in understanding,
Permission of offences leads the game to perdition,
Loading stones is optional are tests to instructions,
Repeating the same process is poison that entangles,
By taking offence and seeking comfort you give power to the other,
The vision of a narrow world gives birth to cruelty,
Ambition blinds the human so as not to fly,
The rituals in obedience put chains and bars,
Losing responsibility puts obstacles without salvation,
Whispers take you away from paradise forgetting to sow,
The habit is retrogression that swallows your identity,
Immensity is a divine component for freedom.

OPEN YOUR MIND TO THE HEART

Master the thoughts or they will devour you,
Under control we serve organisations that distort,
Between in-between to produce obedient slaves,
Without dependency the property that distorts,
Weakness leads to serving Satan forgetting God,
Tricks are the process from selfishness to freedom,
In resentment, pride is a debate for freedom or jail,
It's the devil's swing paying authoritarian tribute
Fanaticism is corruption to have authority,
In horizons the monopoly of truth does not exist,
Between anger and selfishness, hope is enslaved,
Reflection awaits the one who enters the forest,
As the river flow continues to win the race,
Standing on the shore could reach the goal further,
In the area of courage and valors greatness is discovered,
By visualising a destination the present is determined,
The worst thing about being able to see is not having a future vision,
Ideas are key when they become ideal,
Accepting risks is where we grow and evolve,
Regret in confusion is defiance of great warnings,
Stumbling blocks teach not to fall on the same stone,
Setting goals is a necessary educational priority,
Living or existing is the food that unites soul and spirit,
The choice is to follow the heart for plans,
Anger hurts ending in laughter and closing stages,
Control of the shadow is from within free will
Some pretty words may have sugar,
Other hidden words may have poison,
You have to be happy along the way, not just at the end.

THE RADAR OF YOUR SELF

A masked species seeks out of the labyrinth,
Do not force and everything will flow, do not speak and you will listen,
The man with a project always activates a dream,
With simplicity a triumph can overcome failures,
All attachment is beliefs that limit memory,
Frustration pleases the ego to break free is a challenge,
When waking up from a dream there is no God in the invisible,
Nature is everything to follow the path,
By guiding your gaze the steps become firmer,
Learning too much prepares the mind for choices,
Suffering enough there is no panic in stumbling,
When the same thing is repeated, reason does not understand it,
Everything has an arrival with an end to the written story,
The wheat seed sprouts in connection with the seasons,
Leaving the hive transcends being responsible,
Requires no-begging rules for advice,
Cured patients must erase attachments,
For decisive prevention is to trust instinct,
To look up slowly is to show the way,
Feeling united to heaven an infinite embraces the soul,
Because attracting life is emptying pending burdens,
By opening your eyes you learn more than opening your mouth,
It is good to thank the wind for what is carried in cycles,
When the storm passes by surviving he wakes up,
Finding in the footprints that fears are overcome,
Everything imaginary with enthusiasm will always happen,
To reach a capacity you must pass a test,
Faith moves mountains but love moves universes,
Don't stop hope is the radar of trust.

HUGS

Looking up the wind caresses some branches,
They are huge trees that embrace the air,
With majestic sounds between leaves they kissed,
Some squirrels joined to feel his hugs,
They sang with the sounds of birds and landscapes,
As they rounded a path some children met,
They ran when they saw their steps on the peaks they embraced,
His innocence feelings were the glows of dawn,
Walking through the town a bridge welcomes lovers,
From their sweet currents they reflect some hugs,
It is the brightness of young people that are wrapped in songs,
Opening an ancient door a smile appeared,
Someone with a tired image raised his arms joyfully,
When he brought his cheeks closer his fragile health was strengthened,
They were crystals of time that shone when cleaned,
Between friendly hands all cracks heal,
In a park some jumping dogs wag their tails,
With their eyes of emotions, hugs are giving away,
Says the sun and the moon with the stars embrace,
Winter says to autumn that a hug protects them,
To continue the processes with the peace of the Universe,
Says spring to summer let's enjoy colours,
Where birds are born and plants welcome us,
Each poppy flying with its energy carries hugs,
As the wind from above passes with its caressing air,
A few hugs should be the main prescription,
How the water refreshes the body with its sweet embrace,
It is like this all his life from birth and when saying goodbye,
With a hug upon arrival and a thousand caresses as gifts.

TELEPATHY

Closed world between numb and fragile senses,
Fluorescent electromagnetic waves without perceiving,
They are the paradise of the interior where the sleeping surrounds,
Since ancient times rituals are telepathy,
Remote missions sow the spying capacity,
Its metamorphosis is like the desert looking for water,
The magnificent link with the pineal gland,
Meditation stimulates the open connection,
As the eyes are the mirror of the soul without words,
In the dim darkness potential contact is enhanced,
The protection of the afterlife starts with low intensity,
As sacred rituals heighten transformation,
Dreams have a powerful spirit of encounters,
In spirituality changes occur in unions,
The universe does not understand languages only vibrations,
Miracles are attracted in situations of rest,
The attraction manifests with inner emotions,
The real point of contact is to calm the ego,
Where the word oppresses the free expression of the heart,
Unconditional love flows connection and abundance,
As a feather can leave the absence of time,
An invisible tear can be understood with looks,
By stopping the thought, wounds are tattooed on stones,
There are foundations that only by touching them leave a message,
The screams without noise are emptied at the end of a trial,
The rain are notes that wet the planet's souls,
On its arrival every impression carries a purpose,
Stop time in a music with fresh flowers,
Sphere colours fill the spirit of the universe.

THE ARROW OF TIME

A station rests old forgotten and silent,
A whole cycle traversed in infinite eternity,
A sturdy grey stone bench over the centuries,
Surrounded by velvety and soft green mosses,
Some rocks and dry logs accompany his old age,
In his image he created an art with natural beauty,
Without asking or following anyone, their connection is internal,
Free united to the air with rains that bring greetings,
Some hidden traces can reach the spirit,
In sublime surroundings everything is wrapped in harmony,
When the ego of thought dies, the soul awakens,
Connection with life is a journey to paradise,
Anonymous cross conversations are involved,
Some experiences have scars inside
Entangling feelings a hug repeats the process,
A sense of the spectrum changes a material elite,
In energy matrix just split the trigger,
The hypnotic story is about to change in evolution,
Correcting the past will be tattooed when visualising pain,
An arrow on the road points to the obligatory direction,
A seizure birth is very close to the ground,
A new generation is the fruit for rebirth,
The human appearance is only an essence,
In duality a ship drifts aimlessly,
Days and nights will remain in the tracks of time,
The spiral of the universe dreams with passion in energy,
The birds wake up to sing to him at dawn,
The calls are not prey to the lower of the threshold,
The arrow is the voice of times and it is found and lost.

DELETE EXCUSES

Behind some truths lies are strategies,
A single change can move situation and vision,
An imaginable transformation can be positive,
Responsibility is for a challenge to your own success,
Being conformists is the blockage of not being able to advance,
Between complaints and regrets the target falls asleep,
Good excuses put acts in chains,
Reprogramming the possibilities creates purpose,
A life mission is a continuous training,
Laziness is of the ego that destroys with weariness,
Habits have two phases, negative and positive,
Finding the reward leads to free will,
There are limiting beliefs with opposing decisions,
Banishing conformism the future path is born,
In dreams you have to dare without looking with fear,
The I can't is an implant of old schools of life,
You have to destroy the old book to open a new one,
Changing a word brings powerful purposes,
Changing an obstacle transforms a barrier into an option,
A vision is paramount for a developing goal,
All inspiration begins with a bottom to rise,
A great beginning is history with a positive ending,
Boredom numbs to kill life,
Enigmas are inspiration with decisive investment,
A comfortable path loses emotional adrenaline,
Moving forward is the key to facing challenges,
A better instrument is to feel magic with balance,
Traces in emotions are efforts that reflect,
You write your way, what is foreign is false delirium.

LOVE AFTER SORROWS

When love falls asleep in sorrows with thorns,
Save silent roses for when they shine again,
How much bitterness does it take to greet diabetes,
How much loneliness and resentment to manifest a cancer,
How many repressed words to alter the thyroid,
How many dissatisfactions to cause infections,
How much lack of love to generate dermatitis,
How much want to control everything to find migraines,
How much to give your happy power to others to see alopecia,
The more you want changes and the immunity goes down,
How many complaints to others to greet the arthritis,
How long to wait to overflow the glass and dialysis appears,
How many indigestible emotions to suffer gastritis,
How much to feel without values so that the bones hurt,
The more times undergo to damage the menisci,
How much do you feel the need to cross hepatitis,
What will be the abandonment dose for obesity,
How many mirrors are needed to find the self,
How much to look outside all that is inside,
How many deceptions it takes to learn to live
Where is the limit to say enough to the pain,
Dare to make changes, everything starts in one,
You can flow like water when you get the spark back,
As the eagle renews its plumage in the mountains,
Suffering strengthens the soul and enhances flight,
You just have to be born again and relearn everything,
The dream comes and repairs the awakening comes and applies it,
Love and sorrow exist, the application is in the owner,
It is time to loosen ties because the heart is free.

IN A SECRET GARDEN

Some stones hid a flower that was sleeping,
Where the passage of the rain gave him a caress,
A little sparrow bird flew telling old stories,
When cold shadows appear, it hides its plumage,
Every beat of the sun I smiled to give glory to the day,
From a starting point we are all the teachers,
Falling is also balance, you just have to get up,
Learning to live together is to make what is difficult easier,
Experiences are lessons that are reflected in mirrors,,
We are not poor or rich or more special than others,
We are understanding of the encounter that shines inside,
The drums hear sounds to realize sadness,
The aroma of the grass envelops magic with freshness,
Where insect dance has a medicinal language,
There are good follies that dismiss complications,
When I speak to the water, the moon and the sun answer me,
When lighting a fire the wind approaches with spirits,
I like to see the mountains with angels that bless,
The universe surrounds the love of expressions in colours,
Among the aroma of the whole there are different flavours,
To heal the heart is to illuminate to open peace to life,
It is not necessary to hurry the leaves when falling come together,
Between dry and wet new notes can be born,
When you lie down on the ground, time stops in childhood,
You can observe the clouds and at night with stars,
Exquisite fragrances turn into drawings,
A salty and sweet lake is appreciated in its silence,
A sphere reflects pure essence in the lovely earth,
Joining the garden of secrets leisurely falls asleep.

THE PLEIADIANS

Our traveling galactic older brothers,
Reserve of protective guardians of the earth,
The knights in white hold their heavenly kingdom,
Dimensional gates will cover the earth in bubble,
With elevated navigations its light is transportation,
New galaxy like andromeda is in the beginning,
Intergalactic bridges will be able to transfer planets,
Beings with a bright aura that emanate unconditional peace,
Telepathic teachers in constant blessings,
Your planes of consciousness are superior for centuries,
Between energetic frequencies the quantum is reflected,
High vibrations connect with cosmic life,
Between levels changes await the power of progress,
As spiritual guides to channel emotions,
Galactic Federation of Light is your real manifestation,
We are collectives in constant divine expansion,
Irradiation successors in the evolutionary chain,
Beauty of ascending energy for honesty,
Pure expression in the glory of divine creation,
In times of ascension to integrate the truth,
Without fear is to feel the sacred value of blessings,
Discovery the solar and lunar universal identity,
In the galactic and eternal dwelling without borders,
The greatness of the divine plan is cosmic and universal,
Enjoying harmony with the sincere in love,
Your telepathy is valuable with transmission in wisdom,
By wanting to raise compassion the spirit creates spheres,
Planetary transition in delivery to development,
The awakening of universal consciousness is the goal.

THE REPTILIANS

Ancient dwellers of the earth in underground bases,
Carnivorous reptiles with animal food reserves,
Four meters in height are the common traits,
Their footprints are secret and legendary entities,
Tunnels well equipped with ventilation systems,
Ultraviolet solar lighting design for plantations,
Contacts towards humanoids are prohibited,
Material fields are morphologically transformed,
Discreet and isolated in very peaceful coexistence,
Excellent warriors with loyalty and collective order,
With advanced technology in anti gravity ships,
Educational systems are governed from birth,
Shadow elites with changeable nature
Around roots their rigid traces remain,
Firm collaborators by following all the rules,
Ancient apparitions with enigmas for distances,
Manipulation of instincts for supposed pacts,
Telepathic organisers in reckless encounters,
Protective pacts for purposes of military use,
Deals between politicians for control evolution,
Influential governments with secret infiltrations,
Betrayals are dangerous shadows bury crosses,
Leaders of secret societies between governments,
So-called deals await chasing fate,
Enigmatic of silence that sabotage the mind,
Workers collectively seek reproductive ideas,
With gestures they direct the order with precise objectives,
Without feelings or pain they carry firm processes,
The nature reserve is cared for with great prestige.

THE ANNUNAKIS

In archeology they leave traces between the landscapes,
The fallen of temples with reversible directorial,
Originating from the planetary system Nibiru,
Sumerian mythology is your ancient civilisation,
With systems of mandatory monarchs in reigns,
Sages in astrology with precise mathematics,
Galactic warriors with advanced technology,
Makers of the genes for worker hybrids,
Pathfinders in organisation for growth,
Coming from planetary unknown places,
United among their Gods protectors of time,
ENLIL God of the wind ENKI God of the earth,
INNANA Goddess of fertility NAMMU God of oceans,
The most important ANNU the God of heaven,
Great believers of the universe in constellations,
City architects like Ziggurat,
Organisation with plans of secret pyramids,
Cult centres surrounding the teachings,
Great inventors sharing the enigmas,
Cuneiform the traces of their engraved writings,
Clay tablets with important hieroglyphs,
The Epic of Gilgamesh oldest poem,
It is history resplendent with engraved myths,
The Akkadians empire submerged in evolution,
Ancient astronauts leave tracks with records,
The era of rebirth Mesopotamia and Babylon,
The human being is reborn in the mysterious hypothesis,
Remembering the curiosity lost in time,
Genetic engineering is the forgetting of life.

THE GRAYS

Slave workers as among other leaders,
The little gray beings executors of obedience,
Creations both workers with artificial consciousness,
Silent watchers in hidden surroundings,
His telepathy is instinctive connected to the universe,
With implant devices in higher dimensions,
Humanoid fluid seekers for nutrition,
Fountain process necessary for cosmic pleasure,
Thieves of earthly hormones for their procreation,
DNA reconstruction by energy changes
Kidnappings and abductions their greatest goals,
I experiment with humans in the hands of powers,
Clones by opposing commanders in constant vigilance,
Scientific community involving the rulers,
Intermediate changes by extraterrestrial technology,
The human soul a mystery necessary for grays,
Intentional intrusion to experience the blood,
Looking for immortality in information zones,
Trapped souls are raised to create evolution,
Shared gene changes in folded creation,
The echoing room guardian of stories,
Reproductive memory deposits in laboratories,
Traces of memories carried in cylinders,
A bridge race is created from changing DNA,
Labs capture altered reproduction,
Implants are for centuries without authorised permission,
Some will be misplaced by measurement error,
Zones are restricted with their separate condition,
Advanced telepathy for memory erasure.

THE ARCTURIANS

Inhabitants in higher telepathic dimensions,
Beings of light and love transcendental to matter,
Protectors of races of the universe for overcoming,
Helping in evolution to higher planes,
Contact is the sentimental frequency of the universe,
A stable environment is necessary for survivors,
Infinite dimensions with different space time,
Comprehension designed for stellar nature,
Consciousnesses to develop in the universal union,
Shared teaching for infinite potential,
Human observers due to integration challenges,
The three-dimensional is a virus with resistant blocking,
The anchor creeps in very heavy conditions,
Attachments trap in moments of evolution,
The confines of limitations tiring the common order,
Something new is waiting to delete programs,
The desires within seek to release the commander,
We are a group of races alienated from the light,
Like a hermit crab must change rhythms,
Universe is constant renewing movement,
Faith overcomes external challenges they manipulate,
The reality is perceived in the emotional corners,
Elections are captive waiting for reality,
To choose the difference is to change the old terrain,
Animals are masters at visualising their instincts,
The first will be last in the planetary ascension,
The portals will open with perceived harmony,
Loneliness does not exist because union is universal.
Respect is superior, it only remains to pursue it.

THE DRACONIANS

Powerful races in high office with harsh laws,
Diabolical red-eye appearances in your image,
With different traces they surround their great charisma,
Reflecting in reptiles between winged bodies,
Its flights are unnoticed by reactive instinct,
Between their strong bodies they carry animal claws,
Looks high on peaks for its immense height,
Very sinister and highly evolved psychic appearance,
Planes with supreme energies ancestral travellers,
Organisers in measures aimed at obedience,
Rules implanted with dying massacres,
Dictators terrifyingly opposed to peace,
Galactic beings in constant terrestrial telepathy,
Intentionally harmful black magic rituals,
Devastating the solar system with a chosen danger,
The room of time between crystals observes,
On the other side of the mirror parallel universes unite,
Alpha Draconians are great conquerors,
Star travellers scattered across the galaxy
From the constellation Orion Rigel and Capella,
Ancient wars for race modification,
Seekers in enslaving the weak in thoughts,
With altered consciousness patterns are manipulable,
Archangels of antiquity in constant regression,
Imperialist models with innovative telepathy,
Secret observers with jamming plans,
The hidden of genetics is the prestige to the challenge,
Your hidden simple world is original and sacred,
Silent galactic universe is continuous spirit.

THE ARCONS

Gods in rebellion for earthly worship,
Wrapping calm to control hierarchies,
They release sufferings with their protective alignment,
Ordering the rules of the game is to find the origin,
Strengthen ideas so that the world does not explode,
There are chosen for each element in dominance,
By orientations they are protected with implanted pieces,
For channels they will organise the strategies,
Sharing the visions of intuitive development,
Between the Towers there is a traveler with a free destination,
A celestial being embraced by the distant stars,
Flying by nature of divine mercy,
Between spectrum there is an arch of justice and strength,
Rulers of souls to reincarnate again,
Holographic creators where they attract energies,
Angelic beings directed to human balance,
Alarm clocks of potentials to transcend,
Watchers of progress for a new dawn,
The ascension is paramount in the magical mystery,
Cosmic gods with mysterious variable features,
An alliance beyond universal linear time,
Angelic beings with traits of emotional harmony,
Magisterial mythological doctrine in divine influence,
The spheres carry the enigmatic spark of wisdom,
Among the illusions there are traps with lost rhythms,
Ancient Gnostics with mystical intuition of the spirit,
They are cleaning crew where the ego obstructs,
The angels in rebellion were extracting laws,
The universe of flames was the mandatory flood.

THERE IS NO SINGLE GOAL

Disregarding defiance alters the leader's order,
Creating the kingdoms puts minds on a single goal,
Society with forms are directed with deliveries,
Parasitic consciousness dominates the conditions,
Ignorance is an evil thought to fear,
A sheep nation begets a government of wolves,
The virtual is overwhelming so as not to open a mind or a mouth,
Slavery stretches for all to kneel,
Separations are imposed from screens,
Points of attraction trapped in dormant stages,
Concerns united in complacency,
The bloody mind game no longer uses perceptions,
A control can gain access by absorbing resources,
The impulse of the agenda is the octopus technique,
Memories of kindness are forgotten,
Smiles are signs but almost without reality,
Today pretending is the easiest gesture of hiding,
Without exaggerated effort they consider the difficult easy,
Pride provokes a distant and disoriented treatment,
Contrariety of reason disguising the truths,
Visualising the ancestors is the essence of nature,
Creating peace for tomorrow is raising united trust,
The expression holography must change the imposition,
A blank sheet should write the new lesson,
Choosing makes a positive difference in development,
Body is important and I was attached to the vocabulary
Eating and being quiet is the key to not remembering,
The infinite waits to release programs,
Being and not looking there is the difference.

CREATIVE SOCIETY

The directing focus to meet the deviated axis,
The distance that curves the openings of destiny,
The shape of progress raising its hand in support,
A short symbolic teaching needs to be felt,
Consumerism format traps freedom of expression,
A continuous wear and tear lies in the gazes of wolves,
Disorderly laws without guidance of understanding,
Preoccupation with deceit runs to salvation,
Survival is the format with beginning in wars,
As greed and pride need foreign territory,
Destruction is on the corners for following the leader,
The pacifist waits to change dominance,
A deep transformation seeks continuation,
The creative parable is joining moral teaching,
Symmetrical lines looking for the points of branches,
New education is needed to gather wisdom,
Ideas fly by for decades and do not stop,
Projects come and go but none is established,
Desires are implanted with few values,
There are resources in the system how difficult are the changes,
Additions in customs leave heavy chains,
A comfortable image makes the exits invisible,
In cracks lives belief with the enemy ego,
As you start to bottom out the dimension looks deep,
You have to distinguish the listening from the dark calls,
Pride distances itself to wound the heart,
To think that we are not something is to limit capacities,
When desolation takes over the memory is affected,
A lantern is necessary to guide the tempest.

EVERYTHING CAN BE IMPROVED

Thinking that you live in scarcity converts rivals,
The abundant mind shares all the best of being,
Violent intentions unbalance instinct,
Jealousy and greed do not share and drown,
Anger and fear engulfs until the belly swells,
Getting lost in a story makes life smaller,
Generating possibilities is putting a beacon to destiny,
Unanalysed perceptions confuse beings,
Delivering shared knowledge is harmony,
The effort and commitment remodels personality,
Managing thinking leads to training,
Emotional kidnapping is a jail of the past,
Uncertainty is a challenge for survival,
The impulses with faith are principles that have values,
A real courage is to keep walking without a map,
Interpreting to grow lifts the crumbled,
Revealing oneself against what is not understood opens a beyond,
The will mold the brain to level up,
Serenity with the positive is a constant dawn,
A sense of humour is essential for strength,
Talent is created and developed with inner passion,
In ashes of pain there are silences for efforts,
With reflection in nothingness, one is reborn in silences,
Opening to infinity brings dignity with gentle support,
Confidence impulses come in due course,
Confusion and pressure is a vulnerable passenger
To assume the shadow is to overcome the fragile in emeralds,
Being admired for heritage hinders the environment,
You can be extraordinary without being perfect.

TAKE CARE OF THE WORD

The hypnotic morphogenetic field to be activated,
The frequency spectrum of the healing cord,
As a compliant trigger for harmful frequencies,
The existing divisible matrix information ellipsium,
An attentive sleeper with saved energies,
The traveler of the gods and the devil in hiding places,
The blessing coupled with the curse of the flames,
The rose with thorns with the petals carnations,
The verb made real for construction or destruction,
A civilised judgment kiss for bitterness or sweetness,
A predator among jasmine in the rain and the sun,
A writer without a notebook for fantasies of dreams,
An apparent traveler with interests or intentions,
A wound reliever to lift or defeat,
A door opener or window closer,
All communication is waves with emotional Finns,
Bridge for birds like plants listening,
Obstacle to challenge or development for growth,
Feeling united understanding makes the spirit grow,
As the story of everything that goes up goes down,
The attraction is attractive when jumping in divine rhythm,
Silence is the coach of understanding voice,
An emotional balance begins by feeling the opposite,
The trials bring back the directed circuits,
A ladder to progress is a lesson for feelings,
The rush with the noises make the words sick,
The encounter to understand is evolutionary will,
The mind listens to the ego without listening to the heart,
To listen, your brother leaves the ego in another seat.

THE BATTLE IS ITSELF

There are difficult but not insurmountable problems,
We are all heroes of our own history,
Serenity is like a compass with rebirth,
Appearances do not hold infinite happiness,
All potential is in valuing and defining yourself,
The best owner of health is the happiness of loving each other,
Giving the power of thought is the key to dying,
Forgetting dreams due to failure is the biggest obstacle,
Striving in the face of challenges raises the peak observed,
Those who believe in their own worth achieve dreams,
Getting to what you propose is not by someone else's opinion,
Everything begins and ends in oneself by persisting,
To live is to think in greatness and in all possibilities,
Impressing yourself is an experiment of courage,
Only you are responsible for your own happiness,
There is no one outside to own the future,
The only person responsible for awakening is yourself,
Being free is that in your decision no one can intervene,
Emotions are the feelings that we reflect,
The courage to overcome obstacles is to try again,
The human chooses with the heart and justifies with reason,
Arrogance is thinking that intelligence is being right,
Exploring in innocence is the best harmony of the soul,
All change is a challenge to analyse in consciousness,
Love can see the other different but not distant,
Listening and observing is appreciating the universal spirit,
Compassion is doing something with love to help,
The fulfilment is something to fulfil in lie,
Freedom is deciding to have a present with a future.

GENETIC MODIFICATION

From wheat to human DNA is cultivated,
The life experiment to reconstruct the features,
Sequence map with instructions to kidnapping,
The ordered frequency in search of survival,
The cores are paired to rewrite the code,
From something fluorescent life an artificial elite,
CRISPR technology is already a cell of the great system,
Limit moral ethics and conditions for discipline,
Human behaviour in norms to be directed,
Set of values for study communities,
The industrialisation of cyborg genetic progress,
Allies are few for interests in the occult,
Design is programming the material of creation,
A future operation for large experiments,
Modifications are key to creating hybrids,
Development of organisms destined to submit,
Data memory altered in higher process,
The embryos are chosen with superior traits,
In laboratories challenges by artificial intelligence,
Private chain is key with unconscious identity,
Control is the goal without privacy or decisions,
All will be scheduled for common surveillance,
Virtual values satisfy more than reality,
Without freedom there is a shield to punish,
Without decisions, emotional disorders are transformed,
Something will be determined by the past suffered,
To breathe again is to be reborn from a deep change,
Systems are destroyed and it rises to a higher level,
An all-seeing eye will be authority with no exits.

MONEY MONEY MONEY

Birds of the same plumage fly together without confusion,
Passages from the most comfortable to the most miserable,
Resistance identity is order for poverty,
The implantation is education from childhood,
Upon discovering that the elites form a corruption,
Government schools is for the vision of employers,
The people are poor for following teaching lies,
The rat race wraps secrets with division,
Constant hard work is the intelligence prison,
Economic stagnations are bad learning,
Taxes condition employees to target fear,
Release heavy customs that bind to the past,
Financial freedom is trained with good principles,
Education is a response that transforms trust,
Spending time on resources are key to development,
Visualising the successes is delivery without stopping the way,
A triumph is in connection with the interior in peace,
When you think big the wonderful ones come,
Listening more than speaking opens doors to understanding,
Risks are important they are part of objectives,
Failure is not an obstacle, it is a lesson and growth,
There are no excuses to reach a goal,
An entrepreneur guides ideas for power,
A hug to the profit is to share the ideas,
Winning and winning raises towers at distances,
A tool is important in development,
Life is more important than thinking about money,
Educational wisdom makes realistic innovators,
Money is important to jump into the challenge.

NON-EXISTING CODE

The phase is a very analytical episode in existence,
The series are already films with entertaining objectives,
With isolationisms made and wandering fantasies,
The elite sealed in the dome so as not to leave the field,
A mechanism encloses the flame of active control,
Between pleasure and leisure the human is trapped,
In the highest the cult is the most exact deity,
Negative primacy surrenders to the great fictional system,
Something real with fantasy keeps challenges stable,
Clones are raised without limits for life,
Biology will be the matrix with a very obedient rhythm,
When time limits reach celebrations are imposed,
The carousel is a celebration to animate energies,
Satanic rituals for archons that interfere,
Prison farm is already physical and chemical plane in clones,
The biological births will be stories in years,
Smart cities are without isolated exits,
The Watchers are ruled by talented hybrid cyborgs,
A religious shrine organises flight of souls,
Hibernating beings are the roots of the dark game,
Telepathic control is the source of the implant microchips,
The new age will be led by masters of karma,
The seven elders will be the supreme high court,
Beings open fire in dimensions that hinder,
The control will be hierarchical with military levels,
The costumes are unlimited to catch interest,
Proposals for promoting ideal offerings,
The red and blue power has little favour for the chosen ones,
The supernatural is governed by considerable order.

THE VIBRATION OF THOUGHT

You are not only what you achieve, you are what you overcome,
Knowledge begins in the interest that amazes,
The moon reflects to the lake to shine in the eternal,
A rose leaves the moment in the peaceful plant,
Opportunity is the door to infinite opportunities,
By opening without fear, calmness is delivered beauty,
A few tired drops sigh in the air of the breeze,
Fragments bombard us labelling them is selective,
The intellect analyses imposes the decisions on the objective,
The eternal present is a fleeting environment of freedom,
The truth is the mother of lies with excuses,
In failures the hero never turns back,
The insecure mind lives in constant justifications,
Courage in confidence devours the monster of fear,
The environment emits thoughts, particles and waves,
Vibration is energy with determining frequencies,
Where excesses arrive the causes are dangerous,
Depression is grief that sadness seeks to heal,
Stress is the overwhelm in the present moments,
Anxiety is the future that is desired and feared,
To be happy is to be able to conquer each other from separation,
Identity provides views of shared affection,
Courage and discipline is recognising mistakes as lessons,
Every mistake leaves a teaching,
All teaching leaves an experience,
Every experience leaves a mark,
Everything is part of virtue in the field of experiences,
Recognising that we are part of the problem brings a solution,
Children are the mirror of universal truth.

A WALK THROUGH LIFE

To be present is to accept the memory calmly,
To join the beats is to commit to the interior,
Every day is an experience for more responsibility,
Between past and present we are the director of the future,
Legends of yesterday are answers of tomorrow,
The hero's beliefs are stories of reality,
When coming out of the hole the brave in eternity are born,
Survival connects lost instincts,
As a thought is unknown territory,
With values the walker knows the limitations,
Conscious knowledge in harmony attracts,
Trials are waves of challenges to face,
Between desired and changing challenges are endless,
Feeling reality is the supreme quality of life,
After the light is turned on it is the most real world,
Where sudden rubble lies there is some treasure,
Behind the images there is a universal force,
Everything imaginable is unreal, the elevated is honouring,
Wisdom spreads on planes of consciousness,
Every event is the infinite between threads of extension,
The best moments are always on the move,
Deep memory is with the spirit of forests,
The urge to conquer loses glamor and nature,
The search is an inner and transcendental journey,
The first step of alchemy is to free yourself from the past,
All freedom begins in innocence and expands,
The end is the beginning when the outer search ceases,
The spheres of being are like the petals of a flower,
The mantle of the firmament is the Crystal Cave.

THE AIRPLANES SAY GOODBYE

Flights remain in history due to price increases,
The train travels of dreams between seas and mountains,
Magnetic propulsion is delivered in revolution,
All power united with magnets is impregnated,
The infrastructure evolves in constant levitation,
The futuristic sleds destiny between magnets and rockets,
With a click of the mice the challenge unites gravity,
Between the vehicle and the track the crew is energetic,
All pressure is exact the maglevs is technology,
The futuristic ultra fast to successful development,
Between hyper-loop tubes a universal flight rises,
Floating capsules in landscapes without noise or stumbling,
Sports virtual adventures accompany large windows,
Sensors open the door for the power of progress,
The image of the future is generation among drones,
Uber flying taxis pass the fax night and day,
Magnetic levitation floats is shimmering shine,
Fabulous cities without traffic alterations,
Convertible cabins all transportation is digital,
All autonomous truck in elegant transformation,
Artificial intelligence from vision to reality,
In such emergent waves the robotic is like brother,
The metamorphosis of the world is computerised origin,
SpaceX interplanetary SYSTEMS bound for Mars,
Life in special seasons is a real objective,
The rebellion of the machines is universal exploration,
Era of virtual assistance installs a joyful gesture,
Enthusiasm involves neuronal imitations,
In every metallic meta there is a genius with programs.

ONE ROAD ONE RAFT

We are crossing life on the train of death,
Seeing how he progressed ends every generation,
Through the fresh waters of the jungle navigating between occultism,
Deep sensations drown in barefoot glances,
Between fierce shores, cracks separate rules,
Only in murky waters are there blind people who turn off lights,
While in serenity the face of the self lights up,
The road is a goal the illusions only the echoes,
Many flags with fears separate appearances,
A balance is born in the firm and trained mind,
When the shadows clear an eclipse appears,
A magician follows lessons without trying to live them,
Guides blaze trails between bonfires a circle,
The sinister is a hungry power to sink,
Beyond the mind petals envelop the soul,
Memories turn dreams into harmonious intelligence,
Behind the curtain are some isolated capsules,
There is an eternal traveler inside is the meeting,
Walking through the forest some feelings arrive,
Wild plants talked of hidden loves,
Sometimes there is a stream and fresh waters,
Where when dipping feet some fireflies smiled,
A navigator of seas with the tide adapts,
Between the waves and the calm the rudder takes its rhythm,
To travel all the roads is to not reach any,
Do not get distracted by moments that miss objectives,
Close your eyes to crying is the one who purifies and cleanses,
Waking up the sleeping lion is freedom to live it,
Between the road and the raft the boat is the same.

MY MAGICAL SHOES

Some hawks told how an eagle hunted,
Raising imaginary whale and water furiously stirred,
Mountains with snow shine like a rainbow,
They say that when you climb in his mantle you will come down with joys,
Walking in labyrinths talking to the stumbling blocks,
Walker there is no path, this is visible when walking,
Between night and day the peaks change colours,
When walking through the desert a treasure is resplendent,
It was an oasis with freshness giving off lilies,
With intrigues I sit under the shade of bushes,
Looking at the sky the sounds of sirens converse,
Giant trees hug each other by the branches,
Between energies they tell that they are brothers of stars,
As gardens of the world they belong to the universe,
Leaping among the rocks some sounds whistled,
It was the wind of the seas that clapped with the breeze,
Dancing through the meadows some storks sang,
They came from magnolias with exciting scents,
Down a path, butterflies shine down,
They alight in harmony where gardens flourish,
In their flights they remembered to be born is to follow to infinity,
Up a mountain range some horses galloped,
With grunts they lean out to offer a trip,
Going around the sandy grounds, camels appear,
With their long necks they neigh and with their eyes they attract,
In a dog race some cats settled down,
The winner of the game were the felines that flew,
Under the moon and the sun the memories are still young,
To immerse yourself in the steps of magic for a while.

REVELATION PROJECT

Peaceful progress on a shared path,
Higher knowledge from other planets,
Propulsion of strong advances to improve economy,
Promote exploration without weapons that are harmful,
Peaceful cooperative search with other cultures,
Aerospace threats from political persecution,
Blue book process plan with chained belt,
Armies are reinforced with the sixth branch to combat,
Back off the dragon crew for private plans,
Spatial encounters from horizons exploring,
Exploration and pyramids where Antarctica dawns,
Network channels in communication around the world,
Strange and mysterious events at Fuxian Lake,
Relics and foreign cities with an alien base,
Time travel will be shared stories,
Theories are activated with resistance materials,
Technologies in the system the photons are reflected,
ValCamonica carvings with prehistoric petroglyphs,
Dimensional portals where the oracle awaits,
Jumps are divergent by intervened genetics,
Art remains in paintings with hidden creation,
Where enigmatic sculptures are visible to the invisible,
The healing mysterious crystals in their quartz,
The beautiful volcanic rocks with energy give calm,
Works form talismans to serve royalty,
Liberation in caves with enriching encounters,
The chakras between colours surround the universal body,
Sumerian royal list a prism of royal writings,
From the heavens gods fell to remain elevated.

THE PASSENGER OF THE VIRUS

A monstrous capsule becomes riddles,
To hunt the trust of minds that are asleep,
A red bonfire arrived in a scorching heat,
On tiptoe you walk so as not to step on the ashes,
The secret of a ghost leaves you feeling chills,
With a sad appearance, he says goodbye in the dark,
His flight carries a hidden burden on his back,
In the environment that leaves there are feelings of beings,
Some carnations leave behind sealed tears,
On memories parted without unions are pointed out,
Slowly some mirrors leave pieces without owners,
An eraser tries to go through scar lines
In dreams oblivion is left with fired wounds,
The foreign passenger is wanted at the borders,
Hearts are holding almost kind hopes,
Weariness dresses the eyes in sinister grey curtains,
The warm sun is made distant by repetitive anguish,
Mind thinks aloud, asks who it belongs to,
While weary ghost wears a veil that blinds,
For sharing the truth to calm the lies,
The intrigues are eternal when the gossip is lost,
A solitary parasitic moves in played alterations,
Constant mutations shed sores in order,
Defeating hopes to be manipulated,
No need for a shortcut while the people hush,
To follow the novel you need an objective,
One passenger is enough for the story to continue,
The search is long to fall into delusions,
The virus breaks hearts is the politician lives.

.

AWAKENING AT THE ORIGIN

While consciousness sleeps another heartbeat awaits,
When the source is divided, a duality is created,
The dreamer enters fear creating other realities,
As the particle separates, another world is reflected,
The projection into elements is the physical body,
Memories are erased by listening to other people's veils,
Suspicions surround the inside to connect the heart,
Some encounters are vague, others seek projection,
A sick extension seeks mastery in differences,
A hitch chases fear to remember the self,
A feeling of remoteness keeps sending mirrors,
The plan is to awaken holograms by a new system,
To get off the usual train, resources appear,
Coming home is an encounter with the soul and spirit,
A constant sacrifice makes eternal victimisers,
The loss is rewound with jumps, flies intense,
Accept the puppet of the mind, it only remains to face him,
To camouflage oneself with labels is a great mask of the ego,
The custom is the injection of the repetitive virus,
Separation punishes by forgetting that it is the origin,
The beat is to feel that there are no differences in the heart
When leaving programs the history of cycles is reborn,
Where, when valued, glitter and different colours shine,
Looking up there are links that hinder,
Symbols direct the arrow to the present,
There is nothing without ties because the program is continuous,
The surrender of existence is the benefit of surrendering,
Forgiveness goes hand in hand when facing the formulation,
By thanking life the origin awakens.

THE NEW ORDER LETTERS

Ideas are planned for distracted glances,
Silent steps are reflected so as not to be heard,
Traces are not detected, the play is with gloves,
A few chances put bets happy rules,
The cards are smoothly shuffled in the process of the game,
The elect participate with promises they seal covenants,
Cheating is dangerous with penalties to penances,
A conspiracy in dark-looking glances,
There is no combat of forces, the objective is agreements,
Sinister competencies are mixed with theories,
Dominance by obedience is mixed with the game,
The trials in the run put a poster of silences,
Mystic with illegal is observed in the perverse legal,
The mission is to attack minds only in thoughts,
One feels intrigue that surrounds the powers,
Masks are allowed to point out the guilty,
Among the quest for kingdoms evil is accepted,
Opinions go round the roots of the game,
The team is small for sure tricks,
Mandatory control is imposed at the round table,
Objectives with strategies to not lower your guard,
Preserve the imposed agenda to be well governed,
Pass the iceberg calmly for fear of being found,
Fourth power to progress for sinister nightmares,
Removing obstacles is essential on the cloudy path,
Deep dreams lose riches for waiting,
Promoting garbage a numbing smoke floats,
How can the Nile river fall to the north of the Mediterranean,
It is the enigma question when surrendering in cold play.

THE MAGNETIC FIELD

Where the overall effect interacts with the power,
Thought interferes in united phases in masses,
Each movement to progress accompanies the forces,
Thoughts fly by attraction of words,
Feelings affect shared environments,
With emotional acts the keys create processes,
Visible light goes beyond the space in the environment,
A mental order activates areas of energy attraction,
Bodies envelop effects in magnetic electricity,
Among minerals and rocks, compasses are nature,
So that directed birds meet their footprints,
All attention is symmetrical to the effect of return,
Currents follow attractions by attracting the opposite,
Attitude with encounters are to decipher enigmas,
Two opposite poles are attracted by philosophy of life,
Energies oppose and complement your responses,
The always opposite duality is a phase of development,
Challenges attract because daring is a challenge,
In calm and movement the effects balance,
As in the cold you tremble in the heat you perspire,
In the existence of order night and day are brothers,
As the law of attraction good and bad returns,
It is the dance of life with the song of the universe,
Existence is transformation to flow in time,
The balance between force is a necessary control,
Where the poles of the world are perfect bubbles,
All attraction is the charisma that appears suddenly,
Between large searches almost encounters do not arrive,
The unpredictable is emerald with magnetic surprise.

COSMIC SNAKE

Conquests are subdued by fatal movements,
There are turns and abductions with the same crossroads,
Without change there is no paradise from free will,
Legalise ruling forms are imposed without exits,
Higher authorities with lines for contracts,
Seismic earthquakes that do not satan hands and feet,
Manipulated intervention in hypnotisms and beliefs,
The herd indulges in manipulation that alters,
Obedience is the signature of the consent acquired,
The cosmic point does not interfere because it is legal conscious,
The languages are different, the control will be the same,
The unconscious is the victim trapped by others,
By weakening energies, bodies are vulnerable,
Every extreme movement brings strength into play,
Fear with restraints will only be the beginning,
The prison is already a fact without changes of vibrations,
There are open roads out of the traps,
With new systems there are vampires who are addicted,
The frequencies will be governed by rules and principles,
An energetic shield is to change division by union,
History is ancient, liberation seeks a beginning,
Without a compulsory change there is no paradise,
Fiction carries the reflection in foolish conditions,
In the collective interest, entities attract minds,
Between threads is the game with trapped actors,
The paradigm is integrated with financial interests,
Masks drop drop by drop with interest to potentials,
Magic waits and waits in the universal conquest,
Keep dragging the snake to climb to the top.

SILENCE THE MIND

Unites the mind to the heart the word to education,
A persecuted man runs for his life,
Some evildoers persecuted him,
A dark cave houses the fearful man,
Where intruders search for traces with threats,
Supplications rose from the mind of man,
Listening angels calmed their emotions,
Where a spider spins its web at the entrance,
Shadows approached by the entrance of caves,
Some murmurs are heard around here no one passes,
Man's anguish is calmed when he feels his heart,
By silencing his mind the spider went to meet him,
With the inner wall he protected with his trust,
Every morning an old woman gets on the bus walking,
Through the city you see seeds fall from the air,
Says smiling old woman I want landscapes with flowers,
He sows with some seeds that he threw from the window,
Some are foods that birds take to the step,
Others go to the land that lies in the gutters,
Some murmurs sound, the process does not make sense,
The long time comes and an avenue looks painted,
Between the bus route white flowers bloomed,
The old woman in farewell leaves her footprints sealed,
Some children with smiles commented from the window,
Looking at a beautiful landscape with the flowers embraced,
By sowing happy words the reality is reached,
How to savouring life also starts from looks,
Where the mind is silent the universe acts,
To feel the splendour of life with magic.

THE MYSTERY OF THE GAME

Predictions and events clandestine societies,
Without suspects in cases the judge continues without limits,
The game continues the teams are unknown,
The looks are reflected hiding paradigms,
Between faces that seem paradisiac pity,
Actions are strategies by leaders with objectives,
To rewrite stories it is necessary to open events,
Supreme kingdoms rise to coordinate systems,
Cooperation is small so as not to raise suspicions,
When climbing mountain ranges, invisible chains are better,
Falls are a danger for the cause of the find,
A separation is chosen with very concentrated rules,
Bridges are closed when returning to elevated positions,
Silent footsteps and laughter in some ghost song,
Weaken and manipulate with false teachings is born,
Terrify symbolic altitude in key positions,
Destruction with the hidden force of a peaceful weapon,
Distractions for news ideal fantasy for beliefs,
Chilling scenes reflecting guerrillas and crevasses,
They hide in friendly hands two sides of the coins,
Cleaning with famine and plague to reduce population,
Combination in disasters accusing him of terrorism,
Pretension and control to treat new diseases,
Distractions with distances to maintain order,
Epidemics plague fears are the roots of the game,
Smiles become coincidences in rhythmic words,
Masks wrap a sweet dragon of fire,
Colours turn off and on the moon and sun and stars,
Mysterious transcendental game in danger turns.

LET THE SPIRIT SPEAK

As in the middle of the desert an oasis shines,
In the silence is the sage that you carry inside,
The ego is afraid because it is always searching,
Innocence is always born every moment is delivered,
Listening to emotions is the freshness of time,
Joy is fantasy like magic that unites the rivers,
The spirit an infinite journey explodes shine every moment,
Living in peace and creation is an art with smiles,
When cutting a plant, ask its energy for permission,
In each meeting with gratitude, action is taken,
Also the rivers and stones listen to your feelings,
When climbing a mountain there are miracles of encounters,
The spirit is without borders for being a free sailboat,
Good feeds itself and evil destroys itself,
Feel the heart before the mind gets in the way
The body is a vehicle where reason plays,
A movement united to the universal macrocosm,
Among vegetation the spiritual medicine is,
Animals enrich teachings by observing them,
We all go through time walking the same path,
The mission is to wake up and remember the sacred home,
In learning to live the meeting of life goes,
What can man sing if he lives among bitterness,
There is no better hope than to feel the sun and the moon,
When one is lost, it is to meet again,
When one collapses it is to rebuild oneself,
The water that does not flow creates swamps by stagnating,
The mind that retains sorrows attracts disease,
Love has no limits because it is luminosity.

CLONES OF THE ELITE

Powers of top secret royal hijackers,
Finance entertaining famous reigns of the game,
Superior members of great congresses to the council,
Organisation formed in the most hidden peaks,
A control is implemented by answering calls,
The clones are exchange that replaces the herd,
Silent leaders between subhuman encounters,
Secrets that trap minds for slave use,
Duplicate replica robotisation REM phases,
Birth plans with crops for purposes,
Reproductive cells without conscience without identity,
Soulless entities sleep with unpredictable faults,
Fiction in cults are imposed agendas to follow,
Mega rituals and adoration for the beyond in the occult,
Secret world in the powerful ruling elite,
Political armies education medicine all dragging,
Humanity is invaded in great illusion is enclosed,
A flight without a pilot heading for impositions,
Something immaterial to serve beyond time,
Sacrifices and rituals Psychology in delivery of positions,
The smallest with hell between evil and goodness,
Division is the drive to mental challenges,
Manipulation in the process with changes in DNA,
Immersed in the regime the blind go to the abyss,
The cruel system is observed with illusions it is accepted,
Hypocritical the conditions to eat together,
Wearing invisible ties without seeing them they feel,
The development in awakening is for everyone to transform,
Where the universe is harmony life is eternity.

YOU ARE A LEADER OR FLOCK ?

When the facts speak the words are unnecessary,
Leader is the one who struggles to follow his ideals,
He who thinks can not be collapsing efforts,
A potential rises watching with intrigue,
Power is engaging with inner inspiration,
The theory is like a beggar in purple,
Some embrace the rules with no purpose to analyse,
Only by observing colours the flavours are lost,
Steps are lost looking for the footprints of the mighty,
There are hidden labyrinths to sweeten the weak,
Card games bring mysterious dark rules,
Traces differ when puppets smile,
Domains are predicted when victimhood exists,
Some levels are dark for the deaf and blind,
There are towers that rise for the benefit of others,
Facing fears is proof that you overcome,
Where effort is found, trust is companion,
When raising the head the body follows the steps,
There is no evil that does not arrive for good, says the spirit to the soul,
It is only for the traveler to know that he owns his book,
There will never be an eraser to erase the past,
There will always be a good pencil to rewrite the future,
Every mind is a garden with its inner roots,
The outdoor plant feeds on its nutrients,
They are from flowers are where you find your love,
Where metamorphosis is part of the encounter,
Tells the story of life dare to overcome obstacles,
Chasing the one who has grown up you forget your being,
Chasing your instincts in your heart you can see yourself.

MIND TO SUCCEED

This trip is a story with very old pages,
The less bonds we will be, the less slaves,
Living without reading is dangerous forces you to believe what they say,
A change is not with violence, it is with education,
Where it envelops everything with the fragrance of forgiveness,
The resistance phase is pioneering in the plans,
In emotional tension the limit is a beginning,
We are all more than what we see by trusting the self,
The waves heal you hurt when feeling calm in the present,
Thoughts like waves in the sea become,
A diver plunges his instincts into enigmas,
By rehabilitating the mind you are not swept away by the currents,
Being a jurist of causes is not equality, it is effect,
Understanding avoids continuing to cause failures,
Not expecting change in others is knowing yourself,
Whoever loves you will love even your worst flaws,
Who hates you will hate even your best virtues,
The best apology is a better attitude change
Loyalty is returned with discipline from the heart,
By loving yourself a romantic life begins,
Take care of your body is the best place where you live,
Being happy is simple how difficult is how to become simple,
Who wants to do something finds a way,
Who wants to do nothing finds the excuse,
In life you learn, you grow and discover,
Forget the evil they did but not the lesson learned
May the child inside never grow older,
To grow is to face challenges with love and without fear,
To find harmony with the moon in hopes.

I HAVE LISTEN A STORY OF YOURS.

Where a horizon shines and darkness too,
I heard that you no longer get on the same return train,
Because in the future they await the most real caresses,
I heard you don't go back where the heart breaks,
Because dating has taken directions of joys,
I heard your hands let go of the damaged reins,
Because new stars came to embrace them,
I heard that unwanted words have already been erased,
To reach your mind songs of emeralds,
I heard that bad memories you forgot in corners,
Because when a cloud passed the sun opened to smiles,
I heard that murmurs are unimportant subjects,
To focus the brilliance of the glances on yourself,
I heard you don't try hard to pretend you're good,
Because the soul tells you that the truth is inside and easy,
I heard that you do not chase the one who does not want to wait for you,
Because you give your way to the one who comes to look for you,
Heard you don't get back broken pieces of the past,
Because you calmly focus on the easy of the present,
I heard that you do not dedicate your patience to the one who cries a lot,
Because in valuing your sorrows learning is reflected,
I heard that you don't listen to the repeated stories,
Because your ears are freer without extraneous dangers,
I heard that you do not observe puppets with interests,
Because the best mask is in oneself,
I heard you are not surprised by sudden flattery,
Because you feel the reason that is linked to your destiny,
I heard that you understood that the clock does not turn back,
But winding it up again brings divine start.

THE VOICE OF THE SOUL

From the top you can see a path with engravings,
We are all a gift the wrapping is image,
Without being truthful, we must not enter into cruelty,
The communication is the attractive in an exploration,
Diving in an absence reveals a story,
A simple offering carries an infinite embrace,
In the sound of a record is the song that sighs,
How to take care of the actions that become habits,
Meanwhile thoughts are reflected in words,
A character trains to transform failures,
Any impression towards someone is your trapped mission,
The fleeting life is a ray envelops colours and shadows,
History always repeats itself until the lesson is learned,
Wherever you go never turn off your light
The looks with smiles light a thousand hearts,
The hands wrap magical energies of silence,
Where only a caress speaks in signs of winds,
Sharing is the treasure of the traveler on the trails,
Because love is not touched, it is felt and built,
It is not sought, it finds you without knowing your way,
It is not requested, it is given because it is a breath of the spirit,
Looking back I feel the future with gratitude,
Looking up inner strength rises,
There is nothing more noble than to illuminate who surrounds you,
There is nothing more authentic than being sincere in your light,
In winning and losing, rebirth is discovered,
The eyes see others, the interpretation speaks of you,
Peace is an indicator that you have made a correct decision,
Be grateful opens paths blessing enlightens them.

THE MAGNET IS YOU

An inner fragrance speaks to the heart of the sea,
Account that from the bottom there is a path with reins,
Also some dark forces that direct the roads,
Loud signals interfere when falling from the top,
Winds in the mountains reveal their eddies,
Where the birds sing without fear of delusions,
Surrounding some valleys in green aromas dancing,
Some butterflies fly and attract with their colours,
Hungry lions walk through the virgin forest,
When they stop their steps, some gazelles approach,
The footprints of some children jump in free branches,
Where smiling in heights the fears do not exist,
They all attract the rhythm of the universe in their circle,
In sadness rivers come to cry on its shore,
As in anger pain is born that waits in corners,
Sounds are turned off when connecting the silent ones,
Rest is the source that heals all sorrows,
As the mirror is an image of the indomitable heart,
Only appearances scream the looks that are lost,
Adult doubts strike with fire of thought,
Where is the number that exceeds competencies,
Life responds to calls without traveling borders,
As the storm warns with darkened clouds,
The lightning lights the sky and brings noise to the step,
Life is magnetic with the spirit by its side,
The circulation of a system is governed by rules,
The dance of the universe is a simple awakening,
By understanding that life is a passing friend,
All that is received is the cry of the request.

CYBORG DEVELOPMENT

The explainable of the inexplicable fiction in reality,
A digital future evolution continuing to develop,
The rebirth of the species in the jungle of control,
Inspiration from beyond connects the imperceptible,
Between colours vibrations create fluorescent sounds,
Since animals have antennae that perceive,
Between directions of waves the signals are connected,
Every organic image is continuous in projection,
The inexhaustible source of life biological alignment,
A bionic tool gives suspension to life,
Beyond honour reaches a goal of enigmas,
Cyborg is a sense as a sculptor is his art,
Food is like song when it joins its aroma,
The melodies are infinite unlimited perceptions,
Each impulse is the cell where the hardware directs,
Every nerve with electrodes in the unreal communicates,
The rebirth of the species is already creative science,
Where another corner is found and an avatar is activated,
Behind hidden doors a triangle becomes magical,
Tuning in good frequency strengthens acceptance,
Without vibrational change there is no paradise for freedom,
An encounter with events awakens anxious minds,
The illusion is continuous when gathering challenges and circumstances,
Knowing the way is understanding with serenity,
Every space of possibility is a new opportunity,
Dealing with uncertainty is starting each day,
They say hidden words sitting on the seashore,
From a happy cry they say that smiles are born,
Where the human and the tree bear their footprints together.

ARE YOU LIVING ASLEEP?

Speaking to the thought one repressed a fear,
An anxious decision accumulates the aggressions,
Repression of the impatient resignation open doors,
Nerves reach gastritis in negative people,
When sleeping in the mourning murmurs ignite sorrows,
A match in the dark cannot find its candle,
A little bee produces sweet without measures,
Appearances hide realities in oppressions,
Every perfect impression has no meaning or limits,
The absence of self-esteem takes the soul away from advantages,
The core of health is accepting yourself,
Between blind roads appear bars without exits,
Time does not wait for the sad to fix ties,
A slave system is very common in belief,
Material attachments label many ideas,
If you are looking for happiness,
It's because you do not know your fullness,
To learn to be with you is to find the treasure,
Your wonderful interior frees you from deficiencies,
There is no one around, it is supposed to be a movie,
The triumph of progress is living without much haste.
In the footsteps of understanding there are roots of joys,
Ambitious reflexes exceed understandings,
Dreams of white seagulls rise to stars,
Healthy rests in humour sharing their laughter,
Bright colours shine through the skin,
The races are efforts from objective minds,
Do not erase past days are the future food,
When life shakes the spirit awakens,
By not repeating the failures the train travels far to the destination.

YOU BUILD OR DESTROY YOURSELF ?

Without looking around the confusions leave jumps,
The global plan is dominant for central control,
Resources in popularity are dizzying evolution,
One minute can change a conscious decision,
The mind is an instrument with sophisticated plans,
All growth is born out of the comfort zone,
The resources are within the connection is the meeting,
Internal representations are delusions or values,
Strolling through thoughts an instrument of notes,
Some out-of-tune others leave us astonished,
Two elements are chosen by pressing freer wings,
The waves have the truce to know the flight,
Internal limitations hide reality in intrigues,
Walking the unknown changes routines in dreams,
Beliefs are imposed with ties and poverty,
The exterior experienced is the key to progress,
Exploring the unknown moves mountains in colours,
We see the world that we are by chosen principles,
The inner voice puts in judgment the great game of destiny,
Light of understanding trains to create wisdom,
Every opportunity exists when viewing it without doubts,
Good inventor gives rise to the most difficult puzzles,
A dynamic is continuous by valuing the essence,
The key decision is to differentiate the pilot from the co-pilot,
All risk is necessary to reach the new success,
Inspiration is the spirit that risks the scope,
If your big dream does not scare you, it is not up to you,
Reality is kind when it always surprises you,
Opportunity in trust always peaceful the fire.

WHAT'S IN YOUR SUITCASE ?

Grandma says if it rains at home she doesn't open an umbrella,
As in the disease you distinguish who is near,
He says that the wood creaks between silent steps,
To collect the traces that differentiate findings,
He says that the wind breaks the deteriorated glass,
To see in your crystals the needles of failure,
It says that the walls lose magic when hit,
Because in its structure the column is its base,
Says there are locks with keys to lock,
While those of harmonies open with their eyes,
He says that there are acquaintances who crack the words,
But there are strangers who with caresses repair,
Says there are challenges that revenge presents,
While ignoring them all rage is released,
He says that there are dreams that when devaluing are extinguished,
But when shaking the dust a glitter dances in hopes,
He says that some plants never show their flowers,
Because in its green leaves the sun shines with the moon,
He says some scissors cut confidence that they give him,
Because greed withers hearts with smiles,
He says that abundance does not see a poor cornered,
Because only in scarcity do you feel the sores that bleed,
It says that the mirror only speaks if there is a believer,
But he who knows his name does not need the image,
He says homes without respect lose coloured lights,
While a sudden hug mends all the forgetfulness,
He says dull smiles are born from black and white,
Every secret is deception where the abyss awaits,
The cheerful grandmother says in your suitcase goes your destiny.

MAN OR MACHINE ?

A single unified anti-gravity and projection force,
All energy in the field is equivalent information,
Between the lines and strokes are operating systems,
All matter is just the result of isolation,
Projectile holograms become memories,
Good metallic humour reactivates the futuristic demand,
Superior virtual assistants in analytics,
The rebellion on horizons examining the mood,
Human life would arise beyond chemistry,
Programs and competitions thinking in scales,
Neural impulse is emergent simulation,
To regain life is consciousness elevated in singularity,
Human science is an internal combat to revalue,
Normal routines will be mastered digital nomads,
The digital store will be free and imprisoned facility,
Locked in a dream creating imagination,
Minds linked to machines will live in masks,
Between wires electrodes waves will reach the outside,
The brain-machine fusion is lightning and wait,
Conquests of progress in irreversible development,
Coded skills will be shared foundations,
Risks to challenging conditions in a new era,
Competition will make different indistinguishable footprints,
Mixed paths in opposite genetics and wiring,
Looking for the superior between intelligence and strength,
Androids are recognised with futuristic complement,
In the perfect of the shared life and death enigma,
Looking for perfect challenges a new dawn is born,
Curiosity will always lead new lesson to questions.

A PRINCIPLE OF ORDER

Anything is possible, existence is the idea,
The mind is a garden to walk inside,
Some seeds wait for plantations of time,
The perfect plan is to unite the magic of the universe,
Like a tree of its fruit it shares with joy,
Actions are like water as thoughts flow,
The sun shines in emotions with the moon at rest,
Feelings go together to happen real,
The search runs and does not reach the persecuted exterior,
By understanding not seeking a great ground is prepared,
The ties between colours surround the cheerful spirit,
As a sculpture created it is a silence of the soul,
Where hidden art reveals secrets,
The deserved meeting is the creation embodied,
Life is reborn in death when there is never forgetting,
The prophecies are reflected in crossings of observers,
As darkness wraps itself between causes of effects,
A thought is the goal of the goal set,
Steps are keys with traces to the committed heart,
Image tailored progress with afflicted belief,
Helping to grow is perfect when strengthening people,
Evolution is like radar aimed at survival,
In complications certainties are trapped in labyrinths,
To awaken dreams sirens sound in silence,
There are repetitive tools waiting for time,
The goal is the key when applying the feeling,
Passion opens the doors of fixed attention,
Poppies bloom with the attraction of rose bushes,
Protection is the environment where order is principle.

HYBRID INSECTS

Where mornings and nights greet and say goodbye,
Nature welcomes the hidden portal of progress,
Such a varied fate in the hands of experiments,
Strands of waves like veins in directed frequencies,
Creatures galloping as in electric flights,
Danger to solutions is the continuous cause in doubts,
Modifications mutant effects vary arguments,
Life makes its way with reproducing florescent,
Reflexes with strategies resistant to the system,
The transgenic threshold is a virtual challenge,
Diabolical night human skin is the target,
Some inhuman villains between lights are the prey,
Little criminals with three reproductive days,
Among the hot and humid they risk for a bite,
As in two waters life without borders is divided,
Exchanges welcome beings on white peaks,
The skin of the water is invaded in an invisible path,
Stocks without looks, the whole process is continuous,
Caresses of the wind stir fresh waters in waves,
Between the earth and the air, gratitude floats in breezes,
The rays of the sun sigh everything is part of the spirit,
Lagoons, lakes and rivers with gentleness are enveloped,
Metamorphosis is effortless with divine harmony,
Streams rise and fall with songs of nature,
Birds among insects understand each other in sounds,
Earth is a journey with perfect steady flight,
The rhythm of disturbances the human pursues,
The planet welcomes a magical path between glitters,
The system of life only in peace persists free.

OTHER GODS

Each species consists of neither good nor bad individuals,
Every extraterrestrial project is top secret,
UFO ships with measurement of propulsion in flights,
Various beings use changing levels in dimensions,
Paranormal layers only entities understand,
A primitive essence only uses spheres with influences,
In all existence there is always duality,
Knowing consciousness is a simple and energetic matrix,
Dark forces can steal the soul in silence,
Highly developed science is a part of magic,
There is greed for power acquired by aliens,
Simple thoughts given away by interests,
Underground gatherings for peaceful purposes,
The ruling gods of Egypt are history,
Where myths are reality followed by hybrids,
Between reptilians and humans powers predominate,
Advanced technologies conflicts lose confidence,
Hidden groups derived from the past are rivals,
Differences of forces unifying warrior angels,
Galactic existence will be revealed to the future,
Space technologies will open advanced industry,
Contacts from other worlds will be terrestrial members,
New history will be reborn in the circle of the universe,
The watchers move along the paths of heaven,
In the landscapes of stars some palaces have been,
I entered crystalline experiences living beings of fire,
A flood carried away the treasure for filthy reparation,
Constant growth is the memory of progress,
The truth has a thousand doors where the secret only died.

ADAPTATION MECHANISM

The radical systemic threshold for continuous adaptation,
The extraction is biometric for humanity and control,
Dominating the dominant is a game of conscious order,
Deciding is recreation for higher entities,
Virtual reality enslaved by the grays who hunt,
Danger of threats is a challenge to the development plan,
There are intense aftershocks to reprogram the system,
Slavery in digital brains with extraction,
Interconnected signals in the human environment,
Electronic biology to programmed existence,
Genes manipulated for education with interests,
A veil in the blind world breaks harmony to the earth,
Thermal cameras with a vigilance rhythm,
Tracking microchips for constant monitoring,
A dystocia future of the state freedom to submit,
A bleak outlook will live in constant lies,
The world court will be domination in economics,
Portals and dimensions involve dangerous rites,
Underground bases run in attitudes by order
High spheres are characters of hidden history,
Braking successes punish the crew forces,
After a bullet impact the mirror will be smashed to pieces,
There is freedom of expression but tyranny takes control,
A critical thought is suspicious towards governments,
Constraints between slits with ghoulish nightmares,
In the round table where there are cults there are no borders,
The secret order is still the facade of the origin,
Guilds in levels with masks interfere,
One identity is observed another in encounter is divided.

THE INVADERS PLAN

A crystalline stage destined for programs,
In changes platforms are connected interests,
Interconnections in digital brains to the environment,
All the emotions collected in interests,
From the beginning targets by continual lust,
Drone insects for introduction of new viruses,
Drone mosquitoes injecting human venom,
Nano technology adapted to the nervous system,
Digital identity potentially to enslave,
Confusion between humans as thinking machines,
Objectives developed with surveillance without exits,
Control of blood cells bones and mind,
Bioengineering the neural socket including microchips,
A parasite will condition conditions and challenges,
Artificial life is integrated into the planet earth,
The great plan to create a special special to go to Mars,
Like masked in a religion to be embedded,
The sleeping human enters the molecular dimension,
Neural electricity in a cyborg-ruled environment,
The quantum technology transferring in consciences,
Like in a chess game mice running in mazes,
Arrival in hybrid animal and human streams,
An atheistic regime to stay at home,
Extermination is biometric with dark forces,
Using robotic machines is the essential idea,
Selfish claims to extinguish feelings,
The digital dragon sweeping the image of nature,
Going back to the origin demands to find goodness,
There is no final success between cause and effect.

LOGICAL PLAN

A real funny hug at times is irresistible,
In the irremediable there is no bad experience,
A walk through the forest unites thorns with nature,
The only frequency is irreversible development within,
To move mountains we must connect trust,
Reconciliation is creation of conscious will,
Guardians of security are values,
The bravery of the noble soul lifts the spirit,
Rays between colours are landscapes of poems,
Peace is more precious than the image of perfection,
It is sad to be valued more for the appearance than for the being,
To be born again is to find the true identity,
The past is not erased because it is the wisdom of the present,
Before you die, live, breathe, listen, feel and forgive,
Looking for someone to follow in childhood is magic,
The screams are cowards for fear of losing reason,
Life is a card game the player is the owner,
Knowledge is being able to practice a tool,
There is much to learn from a child's question,
There is little to be concluded from the adult's speeches,
Patience is bitter but its fruit is sweet,
We see things as we are from the inside,
Great results require great ambitions,
Happiness is simply loving what you want,
In the hopeless out of control there is an abyss,
Education is the root of smooth progress,
Lonely bubbles start from imaginary levels,
Learn to lose and win rejoice to participate,
The prisoners in hatred are their own jailers.

THE CREW OF FORGIVENESS

Kindness is the best treasure of the soul,
Where the teacher father sun illuminates the mother moon,
The eternal unites life to the land where the irresistible is,
Relationships will heal by conversing with the soul,
How plants are strengthened by recognising unions,
A whole mystery is written and stones leave traces,
The beauty of a gift is created from the heart,
Welcoming darkness caressing the light surpasses principles,
Love is understanding the body that is the temple of the spirit,
Where beating experiences are strengths,
The hero connects from the understanding peace,
Trials are a path that fuels growth,
Some people meet others connect,
Separation is the best time for reflection,
As the inner law is a manifestation of the return,
Alteration always waits at the corner of the bridge,
Being extraordinary brings control to trust in life,
Loyalty returns when it is earned with respect,
Sometimes it is good to close doors to open windows,
When enjoying solitude, better company is observed,
You know your soul mate when you feel calm,
Time forms wrinkles on the face but not the heart,
Life brings tears but it can't cancel smiles,
Take a chance, the good starts with a little fear,
The human library is a walk to know how to listen,
Like a lamp lighting everything begins in one,
Religion is for those who are afraid of going to hell,
In energy, black is the true face of white,
The forgiveness crew is the lever of the self.

INDUSTRIAL REVOLUTION

The invasion overcomes fear in silent violence,
A dehumanising control for separation,
New regime nascent with the lies spread,
Reinventing the nightmare turns into a labyrinth,
Transformation of digital and analog humans,
Life of machines without borders to read brains,
To annul democracy is to modify the futuristic agenda,
A modular reboot for capitalist adaptation,
Reshape humanity for authoritarian means,
Global governance for intentional bio security,
The new regulations on deals for the revolution,
Sitting in the matrix of a giant spider web,
A guide an elite saying for a better construction,
Drag integration with injector of prosperous future,
The promotion brags and lets in the ghost,
System intervention in each facial image,
Reading thoughts influence behaviours,
Centre of the new order dreams of ending thinkers,
Artificial intelligence is part of the integrated movement,
Implantation to advance for bodies and brains,
Unanswered line traces between human robot,
Smart microchips destroying biology,
Very tiny antennae depicting moods,
Synthetic biology on the very near horizon,
In neurones and technologies, the artificial will be felt,
Virtual reality already a fact for greater interests,
Values with a system will be hybrids for the future,
Animals for implant drugs in humans,
Alter the human mixing sparks of enigmas.

INVASION OF NEW STANDARDS

Similar embryos and among more resistant traits,
Evolution and super smart offerings for implants,
Some embrace the path of change, others resist,
The requirement will be a serious polarised degree,
The ontological inequality separates the adapted,
Beyond the process, whoever resists will be a victim,
Confused conflicts will bring clashes that transform,
Surveillance is objective by class manipulation,
From top to bottom a full spectrum tyrant,
Panic-stricken puppets are caught,
Capitalist sharks called sustainable humans,
The process accelerates nature will fade,
The risks are imposed for the drowned climate,
New viruses give greetings to the suffering population,
Accelerator stalled years today the lion waking up,
Minds controlled overnight,
Destruction of liberty and organised crime,
Orders in obedience by new addicted normals,
Obsessive care in health control paranoia,
All game coding will be an arrow without colours,
Each experimental box will have a sentence in the vaccine,
Biometric microchips are the acclaimed strong wind,
The paranormal is no longer a movie, it will be real,
Loneliness on screens and altering the rhythm of life,
The anti depressive joke will be serious for medication,
Seeking fight lies blind by oppressing beliefs,
The questions are you looking for normal past,
Answers are still paused without saying their existence,
Chilling disintegration for inequality.

SMART CITIES

One morning in a circle looking out to sea,
Some rain and wind opens a new look,
The visits are casual, the very usual demands,
Fly a tired thought to seek peace,
Altered world destined for thinking cities,
Where climatic migrants fate traps,
Vegetable towers rise, welcomed with minds,
Multi data tracks between compatible sensors,
Underground gardens for staple foods,
Virtual reality in constancy of monitored steps,
The slave system has no exit doors,
Without private property for the interests of control,
Economic collapse with separatist systems,
In a digitised communication there are only dreams,
Welcome to 2040 I don't have any properties,
Life is lived without money because the basics are free,
Between the return of the digital field there is no privacy,
A flying transport is ordered for visits,
With a look and a thought I can order a coffee
The choices are reflected in fatigue by obligation,
Shopping was historic, there are no stores open anymore,
The world greatly reduced among giant cities,
Friends are the robots among the chained environment,
Time is no longer in a hurry because work does not exist,
From a time destroyed many lives were lost,
A goodbye between delusions I extinguish minds with vices,
Battles leave past with aftermath they say goodbye,
Uncertain future by races that separate horizons,
Without distant movements the artificial is who dominates.

THE IMPLANT THAT CONTROLS

Particles like rain for the new slavery,
Lighting the lonely candle is the best form of control,
Opinion matters so the helm is headed for,
Leading the sheep is decisive to the process,
The fantasy of intrigues is hidden in labyrinths,
The invasion is to unite the unreality with reality,
Sophisticated practices with drug additives,
Narcissism was financed with objective obedience,
The inevitable story is part of the people in chess,
Perfect game plan is that they look the other way,
Abuse in rituals is submission to blind,
It is a system of experiments with a people without actions,
Industry imposed for purposes other than the common good,
Money is objective with the means to an end,
Through finances the depressions were implanted,
An opportunistic division by making new scenarios,
Protection is not believing the campaign media,
Peoples in pride will fall into solitude due to confusion,
An ice volcano awakens in unforeseen events,
Lack of faith will make it easier for the invader to be welcomed,
In comfort man lives deaf, blind and mute,
When waking up the moment is left behind and disappeared,
A second time the loss of prestige will be negligible,
Only a phrase will come out that in the source brings regrets,
Reason dictates conversation, conscience love,
An antidote reminds that the mind is the key,
The energies are light transparent like the wind
There is an ancient map with writing on rocks,
The earth is more than a planet it is a celestial kingdom.

WHEN LIFE SHAKES YOU

What you have in the cup is what you will spill,
Notes whistle in the ear, some are out of tune,
Through the crossings there are cruises with different destinations,
The tests are the signs of the sown seeds,
There is no game in defiance when the train goes to destination,
A proper climb is respect at the top,
Pretending virtues does not shine on the passenger without signatures,
Each one is responsible for fulfilling their fantasies,
With misfortune the race of destiny stagnates,
It is still dawn when seeking wisdom,
Only the flight of courage raises wounded cracks,
The interior does not deceive when the rush pushes you,
Life shakes steps that identity spills,
Actions define you without speaking many words,
Fantasies remain temporary to deception,
In true battle freedom does not imagine,
Dreams are realistic by educating the beginning,
Between the bad and the good, the convenient is chosen,
From ignorance is born wisdom of the present,
As in mistakes lessons and opportunities arise,
From pain the soul is understood for love,
As in worse moments circumstances are improved,
The force faces fear to overcome dangers,
Practice leads the blacksmith down the road,
As the present teaches, looking forward is born,
When you pluck a flower you only like the aroma,
Let a garden shine, smiles are also watered,
How polishing a diamond is life's work
Where footprints are scattered with divine dignity.

THE FOURTH DIMENSION

Between the void and the whole there is purification,
An indescribable place like the lotus flower,
The imaginable in dimensions offers more opportunity,
Some paths between waterfalls will be the transition,
Unavoidable catastrophic changes to the process,
Nuclei and atoms will be construction in matter,
The bodies will be dragged in united formulas,
There are mutations with Elio the properties are variable,
Light obeys particles of physics in transformation,
The sounds will be echoes surrounding unimaginable ideas,
Between colours images come with a different life,
Visionary spaces will sound like pops,
Science fiction something magical prepared in logic,
Cunning like reptiles will be the origin of awakening,
In imagination the features become telepathy,
Communication between silences will calm battles,
Adaptation in understanding will be higher,
Loneliness will be an ancient sense of the sleeper,
Bonding moments will be directed in feelings,
There is no hatred or forgiveness,
Since the truth is to understand each other,
Pain and fear will be easy to find inner peace,
Health improves by learning knowledge,
The interior will be in harmony with the united heart,
The sufferings will only be passed in dreams,
Among errors there is united collective help,
Distance and closeness are movements with the whole,
Differences will not make it difficult to separate races,
The goal of evolution is necessary in consciousness,
An awakening of the spirit rises to progress.

WARNING SIGNS

Trajectory as a species are deer for order,
They seek with experiments modification of old age,
A desert place ignites the calm and the tempest,
Apocalyptic trials seek to create supreme beings,
Some chains of hell hinder the entrances,
The light point matrix is the difference with aliens,
Looking without letting see the soul is common in humans,
Secret bridges seek modifications in matter,
As on the Achilles heel is your vulnerability,
There are traps with no exits when sleepwalking,
Intrigues attract minds the exits are dangerous,
Cults are present for deteriorating attention,
Traumas are inevitable to stay in control,
Some victims move silence is mandatory,
Drugs and terrorism Freemasonry strategies,
Plans are connection with problem and solution,
Mind control is very early childhood is objective,
Teaching is the system with separate memories,
Borderless programmers master masks,
The count is late, the peaks are imposed,
The elect are servants where obedience goes,
Conditions with traumas for feelings,
Some daisy flowers make a decision of lives,
The power play shown in observed cages,
In changes of direction they are like wild animals,
Infiltrated religious break justice in populations,
The coldness is unrecognisable by secret riddles,
Peacefully organised miracles await arrests,
The tunnel passage is a very small bridge.

THE BIRTH OF THE STORY

The rain has fallen asleep on the glass of memory,
Among the poppies awakens the flight of fresh wind,
A cave of jasmine with its aroma attracts,
A serene hermit catches the rays of the sun,
A lost intruder searches the keys of time,
A sage with sweet eyes lets slow breathing,
The seeker is appeased amid the waiting force,
Thoughts of conquering the power that manifests,
Says the quiet sage there is no order without rest,
He who conquers himself is the greatest beloved king,
There is a peaceful path where the stars are found,
The voracity of haste devours enjoyment of the challenge,
It is a disguise to be famous for ambition to acclaim,
In the hidden of anguish the heart is lost,
A doubt walks through the corners of time,
Someone who inspires a book appears on the road,
In the shortcut a meeting asked with a cry,
Where is the answer to find confidence,
Respond free will pursue what you feel,
The yearning for progress is found in oneself,
When crossing a river there are no doubts made to the bridge,
To get to the shores the secret is in the mind,
When you are born there is no difference between day and night,
Even the clothes of the time you do not doubt them when you say
goodbye,
In goal anxiety one is lost in oblivion,
The serene thing about the road is to appreciate with a rhythm,
Very powerful peaks carry loads to the descent,
As the free bird flies the fish sails the seas,
As the wind is transparent, life is in joys.

A DANCE WITH STARS

A walk through life with ashes is wrapped,
Some glittering swans under the moon water,
The silence of the night in a kiss embraces,
From the sun falls a cluster with stars sends brilliance,
Glances of other worlds from seas are reflected,
A rattlesnake necklace leaves distant sounds,
Like a sleeping flute wakes up in joys,
When solitude is populated, hurricanes are pacified,
Between the songs of the wind a harmony moves,
Dreams are companions of heavenly laughter,
Infinite ribbons of pearls in darkness meet,
Ship wrecked when sprayed in lines of the sky appears,
Some bells light up when they feel their nostalgia,
Some echoes in the woods with sweet birds that migrate,
Between the lips and the voice something else sounds in silence,
Fish in the stellar night with the undressed rain,
The howls on the banks feel the fire of bonfires,
Some fans of flowers between wild springs,
A butterfly kiss stands on green lamps,
Simple ring of time without words is understood,
Cloud-shaped colour in journeys of the eternal,
Music with wide nets to blow in drifts,
On the shores birds fly with divine hopes,
Between the stones of the sea cries of waves rise,
Singing roots of heaven when finding the spirit,
A seagull follows me to find the stars,
Climbing to the top chills wrap around,
Lights in a thousand colours with wicks light the tracks,
Purifying harmony with dance of the universe.

INTERNET IN THE BODIES

The trans humanism led to the systematic world,
Artificial intelligence the reality of virtual progress,
Robot and human microchip of the inevitable memory,
Technologies implemented to improve interests,
Between IOT cameras there is surveillance from the clouds,
UFOs and Martians will be compilation in controls,
Bodies in pirates amid changing DNA,
It's internet age for governing opportunity,
From the economy to the industry risk cooperations,
Devices and monitors collecting the private,
Separation of individuals altered by conditions
Fiction is reality for masked interests,
Futuristic fantasy is science techno tactic,
With portable devices to insert into bodies,
Every IBO from Particles to Smart Bondage,
In local networks they will be common by necessity addicts,
Idealists will be advisable how to heal and prevent,
The devices will be a hit as a kind blast,
The so popular invasion will be invisible genetic analysis
Sensors verify minds with emotional traits,
Body function monitored at the interest of intruders,
In the unfairness of the content the address is by control,
The beneficiaries consent to the old dictatorship,
Digital pills will be measures of deception,
Radiation is wireless with harmful biology,
It is villains' medicine, the transgenic will be synthetic,
Increase infertility is the project for depopulation,
The affected identity will lean on reboot.
A reflex of intervention is not to embrace the false.

FOOD IN THE DARK

Roots between catastrophic eras trap time,
Distorted manipulation of the principle coming,
Visual reality is a source for decoding systems,
Feeling distrustful of challenges deciphers hidden doors,
Some levels are stable frequencies to be amplified,
Biology and technology is the same for enemy laws,
The universe is vibration, everything you combine you receive,
Energy is a solution when remembering the identity of the spirit,
By changing the perception, life is going in your favour,
The moment is celebration like a butterfly flying,
Rebooting the system is the connection united with courage,
Applause causes differences, love is more unique,
The last silence is to know the infinite consciousness,
Next program activated in drones for mandates,
Skills dormant by the artificiality of time,
Killer robots arrive while the flock sleeps,
If you want to control sleep you must use perceptions,
Ancient and modern fountains are the same attraction,
We create reality by changing thoughtful emotions,
Life is a mirror that you receive everything as you see it,
A new cancer spread by freedom of expression,
Racial identity is the division to manipulate,
A sensible look but tones are about numbers
Before living we alter information experience,
We are decoders with electrical and digital energy,
Waveform is the truth to get to decode,
There is no free time, the attack is already accelerated,
The active side of infinity must take a sharp turn,
The lion has already woken up, you have to take control.

RADIATION

Shadow of invisible cell unites the ambitious human,
Looks that filter voices for a wounded stream,
In corners some ideas in others only interests,
Distant words approach in infiltrated projects,
Doubts sound in escapes, others think and retreat,
There are moments that appease only for a short time,
A few lost steps keep a people distracted,
Between murmurs, claims for discounts rise,
Circles are very old leaders hold the reins,
Obedience is activated the herd follows the boss,
Darkness blends into glittering colours,
The countdown is activated by not winning the projects,
Peaceful is the appearance for not detecting enemies,
In unexpected corners bars open the doors,
Sorrows come with surprises the destruction is massive,
Running has no point because lightning is on the road,
The train takes smiles that were waiting for departures,
Humans in bitterness change tears into sorrows,
A rebellion armed with masks save their lives,
Other cities complain as they fall into the abyss,
Breathing is slow the screams become silences,
Panic reaches the soul to be understood in friends,
Between abundance and nothingness the heart is observed,
The lies with truths were only the chains,
Standing up for yourself is safer in war,
An old verse says there is no one on the outskirts,
The power in someone else's hand is the jail to your destiny,
There is no better me to meet than to wait for an enemy,
Dance safely at home without looking at your neighbour's.

UNTIL THE VIEW DEAR EARTH

Our magical home among the immense sun,
Nightfall of stars with the traveling moon,
The dance of life with unconditional love
Friend of the enemy with beauty of adventures,
Spectacular tenderness despite so many wars,
Kingdoms come and go with mysteries they leave traces,
Thank you for the multicoloured flowers lighting up,
For a beautiful sigh that is kept and not had,
Thank you for meeting you at such a distant moment,
In the air of the road you have made the days cool,
Thank you for offering the songs with the landscapes,
Animals intended for food and companionship,
Thank you for your presence of divine love without rancour,,
Between shimmering oceans balanced with life,
Thank you for the silence of peace among the waves of the sea,
For the heat and cold for its balance in sessions,
Thanks for the fire and rain for feeling your difference,
Earth and Mars born for continuous shelters,
Wonders of creations between genocidal hands,
Migrant scientists intrigued by conquests,
The walking population without rest to progress,
Decisions is the eternal burden that is carried,
Since energy is not created, it is only there and received,
Hungry in matter they drag thirst in the farewell,
Between microbes and organisms the dance was incompatible,
For humanity that are destroyed by feeling need,
Leveraging works by merits forgetting the heart,
Dying in dreams continues the journey of search,
Wise nature alone leaves yesterday to continue the flight.

ENCHANTED PLANET

Sunlight virgin star reigns for opening hearts,
A unique home in history inevitable to progress,
Between fantasy islands the fairies leave a story,
Forests keep secrets where they house beings,
Mountains look at the skies when the stars greet,
Green valleys with rain cool smiling birds,
Some streams carry the stones for sounds,
Fall in gentle winds, waterfalls with storms,
In a few turns of valleys some storks step,
In the deep dark sea some species hide,
Some coloured fish jump between breezes,
There are some children who play among scented flowers,
Some ants walk incessantly on solid ground,
Howls of wolves are heard in some wild mountains,
White and opposite glaciers that maintain harmony,
Seagulls of green seas in the blue cry out into the air,
The stars with the moon between comets meet,
Fireflies also shine among happy crickets,
Wild horses feel their hair free,
Heaven greets flashes as they dazzle in colours,
Trees give fruits with sweet and fresh flavour,
The sown land offers the food of the soul,
Between the heat and the cold the caresses are the same,
Some happy insects also give murmurs,
Between a dance and song, eternal waves embrace,
Looking back the night says goodbye to the clear day,
Some clouds cross and the rainbow rises,
The cycles for changes are sleep and wake up,
Mother's love houses children with a spirit to sail.

PROJECT ON MARS

Between blue and pink polarities shine,
The gold in the space with crystalline roses,
Passing through a galactic world of dry ice,
Sleeping waves will take flight in warm breezes,
Wanderer without a path will heal wounded footsteps,
Searching for life on Mars is chemistry of our origin,
One more brick is invented with vegetable material,
Cell food replaces animal protein,
Insects are protected for primary consumption,
Fertilisers in process to follow the transgenic,
Cave-dwelling surfaces with protective igloos,
Between robotisation minds become united,
A rowing boat will be the wings of return,
Thoughts develop silences to challenges,
Borders open to heaven doors with secret signs,
The threshold of the enigma that surrounds experiences,
The new cradle that is born of human civilisation,
Cologne for life with opportunity from scratch,
Lagoons will open streams to rise to the sky,
Life in motion where the sphere awakens,
Rains of reddish dust will give celestial brilliance,
Birds of the future are the drones without their song,
Challenges to the challenge is choice for a shelter,
New chapters of history are the expansion lived,
Among emeralds protons will be nucleus of neutrons,
The neutron of the atom in Elio will be the future energy,
An inspiration is courage of the unexpected great,
With a strong crew the adventure is an achievement,
Sailing in cataclysms is a cry to infinity.

HYBRID LINEAGE

Bodies of the same image wrapped in the artificial,
Genes sequestered for the purpose of transplantation,
Opposites in the game of addictive development,
The third time asleep between spheres liquids,
You wait for interests with no sign of a feeling,
Screens isolate questions with objective answers,
There is no obstacle while addicts chase the net,
A selective reflection in isolates hides,
By believing in the higher, advice is disturbed,
Streams of propaganda blind minds to ideas
Tricks like lightning that transform the system,
Evil goodness is no different when looking at other planets,
Absolute power are dreams of ambitious humans,
Driven by targets of beings in other galaxies,
Reflections have no questions must follow the leader,
A dictator is stagnation with side effects,
The thunder was heard for a secret origin,
Voluntary mass minds to follow the elite,
Technology for victims attracts relentlessly,
People of the blind world fall in chains,
Between wheels they crawl through the cracks of destiny,
The cheerleader for help must leap from its clutches,
By turning off the outside streetlight, the inside is meeting,
The law of the soul is manned for constant return,
To restore sanity to the world needs collective help,
A great change is very necessary to see equality,
The mechanical is the engine of the great evolutionary change,
The human is the battle that is devoured in progress,
Heart between metals is like the fire dragon.

INTERSTELLAR WORLD

The new era explodes rhythm back does not go back,
A long course united between the artificial footprints,
When the fuel says goodbye, energy pressure is born,
Connection between galaxies with encounters incognito,
Intentions in conquering bodies of light and other beings,
Powers always opposed interventions by clones,
War in search of food for opposing proteins,
Procreation seeks genetic inevitable experiments,
Other bloods, other traces between fluids and acids,
Opposite worlds with liquid crosses that transform,
Contacts between battles with lasers and explosives,
Little trust between stars the observation is continuous,
Life by calm is shortened by fear of the enemy,
Land forgotten by gases the capsule is the vaccine,
I play a distant universe to the dance of the great journey,
While in constant travel the old wound rests,
The healing of the land goes silent in its fury,
The horizon in events will be the attracted sphere,
In force greater or less the relative is the distance,
Where protons explode energies are particles,
Integrated space mining searches for asteroids,
New mythology reinvents the present of history,
Composition is accepted by mandatory inertia,
The quintessence star for being an immutable element,
It is observed in the distance without ignoring the past,
One side of the field always visualises with the heart,
One runs another pursues to complement links,
A murmur reappears when sewing a wounded heart,
When they heal, understanding cataclysms they vanish.

LUNAR BASE

Dark side and light side in riddles with visitors,
Secret history door with way to the universe,
Natural resources in food projects,
Developing minds in search of the lost soul,
Dimension is very old in the occasional occult,
Matter in bubbles in very constant motion,
Satellite for refuge among its dark sand,
Station orbit for international introduction,
Between ambition a leap into reality awakens,
Resourceful materials open the mind to progress,
Between micro meteorites a maze game is born,
Extreme temperatures in conditions give events,
Where glaciers rest, visions rise,
With three days of travel from friendly land,
Waiting for the pleased moon for a discreet welcome,
In commercial trips colonies will be his days,
New window to the universe leaves traces and enigmas,
In the Martian, the existential is a principle in advance,
Companions of those who came to populate yesterday,
The domes are the guardians in secret exploration,
From earth to Mars stopping over the moon,
Hotels in orbit lie for exploring minds,
Constructions under tunnels with stored energy,
Among a giant design enjoy the moon in its channel,
The mysterious sphere alien to the solar sister system,
Its distant distant origin from the corner of the universe,
Her scars in craters with serene desolation,
The eyes of every galaxy underestimating the intense,
The great lady of the romantic and amazing night.

UNDERGROUND FACILITIES

Secret caves shelters of reptilian earth,
Big cities in advance colonies,
Gravitational light sources due to natural inertia,
Round metal door to the subhuman defiance,
Symbols leave marks other strangers fill wars,
Hostile races open the path of fire in challenges,
Past encounters with cults in events,
Temples for gods for evolutionary attention,
Ancient testimonies pay homage on walls,
Secret meetings are summits of future laws,
Without special training in forces of the mind,
With advanced abilities that are born with telepathy,
Secrets in telekinesis shared by the basics,
Weak human mind accepts orders with induction,
A simple switch what you want done in real,
The consciousness from caves is activated in keys,
Between appearances the permissions are directed,
The tracks are original between cameras and filming,
Long praise and reptilian war marks the separation,
Evolution project is the fight in challenges,
Interests in genetics in artificial crosses,
Weakening the ability to think is the goal,
Bubbles walking through quantum technology,
They leave information inside the progress closed,
The primitive past is a bridge to the future,
The alien molecular structure in information,
Hydrogen air and DNA an inevitable interest,
Sonic weapons between bases will be space control,
Fearless world leaders with galaxies dress up.

INTER-PLANETARY MESSENGERS

Some people act others help with actions,
We can't carry everyone in the light change,
We can all try to give someone learning,
Intelligence is expandable in neural process,
Inventing to reinventing ourselves are dreams with reality,
The essence of the process is an enigma to explore,
A started is reborn to be a sculptor,
The mechanical world radically disappears,
Challenges turn into new magic,
The rebirth says goodbye to the old,
The unreal in flashes opens up in dimensions,
Immersed in the divine is a field free of obstacles,
The multi dimension is not a mystery it is the source,
In old actions the mechanical slow will be history,
The linear will become quantum between opposites,
Invisible doors cover communicative differences,
Planetary seeds enter challenges,
There is a horizon that points to the inner arrival,
Supervision of obedience in a turn says goodbye,
The new jubilation of the people comes in a new build,
The new age will be a dawn of understanding,
An overwhelming schedule from the top watches,
There are upper eons and lower eons between curtains,
The upper eons emanate from the silence wisdom,
The lower eons of noise seek obedience,
The aeon not time is the meditation of awakening,
The prison planet will follow the running course,
The decoding will be Apocalypse of brightness,
Resolution of the biological and technological is the same.

A MAN FROM GALILEE

Embracing the light stars tell us the story,
Survival appears out of revenge for the beast,
An angel of the sword will destroy the dragon,
The defender of life is dimensional free from anger,
Being from natural paradises to create with love,
Without ties it arrives as well as I leave in farewell,
An unshakable race without borders in its oasis,
He does not look for lighted candles or anyone to kneel,
Cheering for blessings not calm degenerates,
Dressed for flattery, the wicked do not cease need,
Adoration towards someone is losing inner value,
Justice goes to the soul by feeling peace in decisions,
Protection is the way where the guide leaves teaching,
Mediocre patients ask for forgiveness and there is no time,
The rebellion is written the opportunity reached the limit,
The ancient serpent follows in its footsteps through the fruits,
At the front the strategies will not cease their course,
Inter-stellar wars raging stone upon stone,
Heavenly armies are the forces of order,
The invisible in nothing are the elders of times,
The dance of the sun will dry the rain for weary minds,
The great order of the supreme will extinguish slavery,
Mass destruction will be inevitable in tears,
The earth in its imbalance will tremble to be reborn,
Abyss of world order opens before the divine,
A white dove will purify the skies of pride,
The renewal will be a hug before the whole united,
The sword of justice will return hearts to love,
The darkness overflows the darkness into emptiness.

IN SEARCH OF THE SPIRIT

The time of the jaguar is not lost in the jungle,
Through the unknown eternal life continues,
A growth along the way connects with doors,
There are levels touching the soul with dimensional planes,
The habit does not make the monk more slippery in the slave,
Two beings in affection, action surpasses word,
Every moment in harmony keeps internal flowers,
Evil resides in good, decisions drag it down,
As the tip of the iceberg defies the currents,
Cruel is to disgust vigilantes without practicing the same,
Chains are lost souls by not finding the key,
Criticising the wealthy loses the soul in envy,
A ship without a weather vane is lost because it is not free,
Without union the instinct remains for its own ambition,
Human lives in search and capture without reaching an end,
There are orders in obedience without understanding the exits,
The company of crows that devour the dead agrees
While righteous politicians are devouring the living,
The soul rejoices to feel the hot sun,
As we contemplate the morning trees with their sounds,
The breath so simple carries the shadow of the soul,
Valuing simplicity is the answer in the search,
In warm sweet hands the life of the soul is born,
The limits sleep souls for spies with projects,
The dynamics of oblivion is kept in hope,
Every experience suffered leaves exits in the soul,
A circle is the compass where a needle begins,
The compass follows the circle and in union they reconcile,
The lie for the truth are the stones of the track.

TIRED OF SUFFERING

In the mark time the heavens are like guides,
Being afraid is inevitable, overcoming it is a decision,
Control over the world will dissolve into nothingness,
The light in a great awakening will penetrate the veins,
There is a chain of events in drowning does not drown,
By focusing on your steps you do not see other people's mistakes,
With your eyes open with dignity you forgive yourself,
Where we pay the most attention, more life is born,
Everything around is like a controller without a pilot,
The evolution is in preparing with an inner control,
Addicted virtual games slow the developing mind,
Trance moments in games are dark currents,
It is important to understand yourself first,
When you hope to find someone to be happy with,
The someone will be your owner where you will sleep,
In the smile to yourself you will understand the real happiness,
By not knowing how to die at birth you will be a poor traveler,
Earth is heaven but also hell,
When feeling the spirit there are clues to sudden calls,
Light, sound and colours are flashes of love,
Memories in darkness do not respond to calls,
The similar vibrates to the similarity law of attraction,
You need nothing and no one when you meet the inner bird,
The journey of the soul is something more than the present life,
Each person in your destiny has a teaching,
Do not wait for the train of time for not walking a step,
Life is a mystery with a permanent intrigue,
Jump in your free steps to make your destiny,
Since between the child and the old there is always the same line.

THE PILOT OF DESTINY

Let the music that sounds and the voice that sings,
The reflections hidden in happy tears,
Between nations customs are involved,
The changes are beyond explanation,
Where there are tears, repressed freedom is wrapped,
Bitter lemons sweeten the heart,
The lessons of the past is school, you do not load,
Tyranny knows no limits to its appetites,
Take care of those interested in your good can be jailers,
Your best caregiver in soul and body is your thought,
Helping the deserving is more valuable than the needy,
Success is a discipline that is constantly practiced,
Treat the body well as it is your temple of treasures,
The profits are in the satisfaction of the feeling,
As good words are healing without medicine,,
A pilot says don't bring your need bring your wisdom,
Before reaching the top, observe how to go up and down,
Never attack problems without first seeing a solution,
Everything earned is defined by the value that one put,
Bad weeds are treated stiffly, not roundly,
The philosophy of progress is to repeat conditions,
In destiny the bitter thing is to feel loneliness,
A sleeping farmer is fascinated by the nightingale,
Even an absent loved one does not make us lose paths,
Among red clouds there are wonderful phrases,
A core of existence grasps the old and the new,
Cycle in two realities arrives in frequency to the earth,
Solar storm in the quantum is the key to the trip,
A veil flies in the air and always finds its destination.

THE THYM

The immunological pillar that rounds your love life,
Energy source by reason of your heart,
Passive passenger companion on your trip,
Emotional teacher listening to your songs,
Tight developer in disturbed situations,
Reflector of the details goes up and down mountains,
The walking energy gland of your forehead,
An illustrious unknown friend in secrets,
Confusing doctors because it is part of the spirit,
With childhood he sings in brilliance, jumps and plays the rope,
In adolescence he shrinks with enemy fear,
The pillar of consciousness with an awakened language,
The call centre produces its current defence,,
Thoughts feed him from being sensitive to touch,
Between emotional struggle weakens its flashes,
With happy images create protective cells,
He loves colours with happy images,
From the sternum awake protected by the thorax,
The inner being of the self which with the hand you declare,
A few taps on the thymus raise sad mornings,
With reflection in reflections his Joy lifts you up,
The solar plexus of time the harmony chakra,
An eternal companion without knowing lives without haste,
Your sensitive understanding with hope follows you,
Perfect nature light without hidden darkness,
With long and short steps between invisible mirrors,
Dreamer in full moons to grow in harmonies,
Quartz crystals protect your emotional level,
Body and nature centre united to life.

GOODNIGHT

An educated mind lights up brilliance by sharing,
Luck is in the faith that does not defeat victories,
Where gratitude reminds peace on the roads,
The arrival of the night finds its fine songs,
With dances between the eternal of universal love,
In union with the stars between moonwalks,
Going up to infinity are other landscapes,
Only the thoughts are talking to the soul,
Some without knowing each other can feel the entrails,
Feelings seek refuge centuries await changes,
At night there are travellers who repair the wounds,
Between the dark infinity you can feel the light,
The soft beating heart asks the mind for silence,
Star-seeds accompanying healings,
Between antennas each one enters his need,
Discovering himself in the self that experiences life,
He begins at night trips known in oblivion,
Sparkling energies surround cozy caresses,
Enigmatic portals offer inner wisdom,
Nightmare encounters transform memories,
Nothingness dies, everything and among the traces it resists,
A few drops of rain recall the existential circuit,
Where the sea flies to the sky to cross land and rivers,
On the essence of the mantle feeds equality,
The obligatory rest will be the failures of beings,
With the good together with the bad, the movement awakens,
To be reborn united dawn of sunsets,
Where inside and outside is constant flow in veins,
Let us leave nights with days to the divine guide time.

GOOD MORNING

Rays of the sun greeting the birds every day,
While animals of life leap through the valleys,
In the sweet dawn there are sheep grazing,
Some hunting mountains recall free stories,
Where horsemen ride among loving deer,
Pilgrims walking among trees take shelter,
Surrounding bushes some cactus forms a cry,
Sunny gleams light up in harmonious caresses,
Poppies shudder with sounds of bees,
When colours shine, some fountains form dances,
Some rumours are heard loud among currents,
Among the nets of a ship entangling some stones,
The murmurs break grace with the choppy waves,
The wind from on high changes sounds into phrases,
Tears of sorrows will be shed in the shadow,
The green grass between flowers embraces the mornings,
Voices enchant the air with the smile of children,
The move is constant with the growth rate,
Adventures leave stories with the traces of return,
The heat is melting the ice of the wrapped cold,
The beasts of darkness are eternal but they die,
In mercy good people leave a stamp on stones,
As the earth loves the sky of the same is the eternal,
There is no fatigue in racing when enjoying your destiny,
There is no loneliness in the soul when finding oneself,
There is no graver condemnation of the lost in spirit,
Let your body guide in wise nature,
Crystal clear waters reflect happy meadows in glitters,
Sadness and Joy are his verses night and day.

THE INTERNAL WORLD

To be free a bliss in freedom knowledge,
Destructive forces will leave experiments,
The great central sun alpha and omega shines bright,
An evolutionary transit embodied the environment,
Galactic planet connected in mother and father,
Minds develop talents in new technologies,
Reinventing itself in the wheel a new chapter arises,
A spaceport within the hollow earth,
All planets are hollow with opening both poles,
Lenticular clouds floating to camouflage existence,
Traveler's of the universe at indefinite will,
Between waterfalls and crystalline illuminated gardens,
Amino Acid Computers Detect Misstatements
Peaceful living conditions enjoying millennia,
Errors are immediately corrected,
There is no disturbance in vibration sounds,
With starships we carry supplies,
In underground cities there are no borders,
Infinity particles are parent genetics,
Every source is knowledge to release the image,
By Contemplating clearly comes subconscious input
The energy points maintain stability,
With the earth in dimensional portals we unite,
Duality is the generating principle of the cosmos,
Agency intends us to be better than ourselves,
At levels of attraction turn off the mind turn on the soul,
The perfect nature is learning for humans,
A step of success awaits to climb the pedestal,
Loving the process is the threshold of the spirit.

WOMAN OF LIGHT

Quantum reprogramming with healing frequency,
Restoring memory running through feelings,
Lovers who embellish with alchemy that captivates,
Patients listening as well as separations,
Creative dreamers companions in loyalty,
Marking beautiful memories in united civilisation,,
Peace of mind in fullness in homes and temples,
Without competing in pairs, harmony is the mission,
Unconditional consistency sharing is what is valuable,
Independent insurance for the intuitive value,
Without showing off anything because the whole is complete,
Another was another world is approaching without recoil,
To accelerate unique souls to harmony,
Irresistible presences with memories in brilliance,
As the unseeded birds of the sky have a harvest,
As a caress of love is a sanction without pills,
The development of consciousness enters with energies,
Connection in holograms contain new systems,
Silent supports will be a flowing development,
Between codes of light to share dreams,
The world is a game of complementary opposites,
Which keeps the flame of life burning,
Like a bridge woven to revive your spirit,
In ceremonies it is appreciated when drinking from the spring,
Share with other worlds without thinking of destruction,
As he who learns teaches and he who teaches learns,
To carry love in victories is to beat time,
Remember that happiness is not sought it is already in you,
Where the mirror of day and night is a hug.

TRAIN YOUR MIND

Don't waste time focused on bad situations,
It generates possibilities something that excites the soul,
For an incessant dialogue that explodes in the mind,
Training reflection is the smart word,
Look inside where the root of progress is,
As a new language and a sport is to choose,
Emotional strength is harmony of the environment,
An uncertain world must overcome disorientation,
Commitment is attracted with self-confidence,
A potential encouragement takes honest resources,
A range of colours has secrets from the past,
Where being brave and daring raises the courage,
The greatness of the interior is sometimes muted,
To invent the future is to return to forgotten knowledge,
The construction to the present is radiant to the different,
What the past report should not be decisive,
Inspiration is the breath where ideas are born,
The right path is not always the easy one,
Laziness and fear are paths to destruction,
In efforts there are colours that lead to success,
The magic recipe of a genius is practice,
Endurance in darkness rises raising stars,
When creating the idea in identity a rope lifts us,
In unexpected openings there are windows to fly,
Good thoughts believe in novelty,
Where the playing field offers opportunities,
The oracle of Delphi between two dawns loses us,
The cage of crickets sighs in delusions,
The inner teacher is the palace of the soul.

CHOCOLATE

No one dies of thirst between lakes with gardens,
Life is a song like art encounters,
Delights rejoice among small and giants,
The temptation of flavours is quite irresistible,
Behind in the dark that attracts the flavour in glitters,
There are dark plantations that captivate and enslave,
Necessity leaves children to forget teaching,
Between hunger and misery there are silent screams,
A fertilised cannibal agonising the earth,
Chains for profit are blind circles
Between bitter businesses the flavours are divided,
Companies hide in deforested forests,
There are no simple solutions while minds sleep,
Neither methods in changes work alone, the story waits,
Production in poor countries without tasting their wealth,
Those above look to the sky in gray suits they rebel,
Hope will break chains through rebellious cracks,
Rebellion on earth is necessary for penalties.
Living are three stages where the taste is peace,
An equality is acclaimed in a book to answers,
Among a gigantic commerce the enemy is sought,
Words fly in ruins walking long nights,
Between cards there are a thousand games as long as they agree to play
them,
Empires between delicacies with bandages abroad,
Goals accepted by paralysis to greatness,
Sweet chocolate in the bitter kneeling his soul,
The expansion is elegant with choice of theories,
Tired centuries unchanged tremble the universe,
A beginning comes to an end by accepting its harmony.

WE ARE NOT POOR

Rancour teaches us to say goodbye to hatred,
As old age hopes to find the child again,
To take care of what was conquered as a slave you have tied yourself,
In ambition you lose your way when you want to fly,
Being rich is not having much, it is needing little,
Flying low in success you never lose your way,
The eagle flies alone for its destiny to be free,
To be poor in spirit is to be rich in heart,
A real friend is like oneself with another leather,
Distances are riches where we play small,
A guitar heart expresses many memories,
Taking risks is a journey to contemplate sunsets,
Wealth is having more real problems not imagined,
How to deal with life with many good moments,
Not to miss out on now is to carry lighter loads,
Wealth is spring when barefoot feels its freshness,
Discover the sleeping mist in the harmony of attempts,
Go back to the distances and tell secret stars,
Don't try to be perfect because madness is a poem,
In sunrises there are brightness as in playing with children,
Without wars or hatred or envy, life looks more beautiful,
If weapons were necessary we would have been born with them,
He who wants to paint does not paint, only he who knows how to paint,
Feeling wet feet in the sea is like jumping into the air,
To be neither age nor colour is to be happy with one's identity,
The secret of wealth is to have less and to have more,
What stops progress are mental ties,
Listen to the heart before the head intervenes,
What is lost in glory is gained in eternity.

CHOOSE YOUR COMPANY

The reconstruction of broken mends the ties,
In a fright a book is opened inspiring as a compass,
On a foreign path the soul guides the spirit,
Learn to become your inspired company,
The crumbs of a poor man when shaking them awaken,
The companion who criticises becomes lonely,
Wisdom is the purpose of feeling a firm ground,
A well of humiliation with forgiveness is crushed,
Metamorphosis spreads wings of birth,
In company with heaven there is no business involved,
Clarity reconstructs the sacredness of time,
Wars abound in the mind in peace there are rewards,
Opening doors with smiles are praised surprises,
The planet belongs to everyone but obedience denies it,
Simple is wonderful as the scent of flowers,
Physical pain shows sleeping rage in mind,
Order that breaks victimhood is eternal serenity,
The blessing manifests loving each other equally,
To love out of necessity is to tie oneself to the enemy,
The glass mirror steals dreams with beliefs,
When getting lost in approvals, the ego raises its forehead,
Sufficient self-esteem builds on failures,
Trying is always a lesson in certainty ceremony,
Helping to grow is to be an example of wisdom,
Justice in inequality is opposite benefit,
The best apology is just a change in attitude,
To be free in the soul is to know how to be independent,
The most important guide is your body when listening to it,
Where in small miracles trees are born every day.

WHERE IS THE KEY

Some people live but die without being born,
When a void is filled, vices say goodbye,
True love is scared of souls not bodies,
There is no second time for a first impression,
For a better world we must smile more,
Heaven is knowing how to play with the two polarities,
A teacher is not made only on the way he is made,
As the storm goes in favour of the sailor,
There is a permanent dance between the light and the shadow,
But one lights up looking in the dark,
The trap of rituals are misleading challenges,
Between angels and demons is wisdom,
Liberation from the approval of others is Freedom,
Attention is an element that helps growth,
Great is he who walks without stepping on others,
In the puzzle of life, do not place pieces without a place,
Strength is not resisting, it is not falling into a bad experience,
Helping hands are nobler than praying mouths,
By knowing how to restrain the tongue you learn to win battles,
Lower the volume of what you hear and increase the volume of feeling,
Fly without permission, the wings are yours, nobody's sky,
Choosing your own path without pursuing is finding yourself,
Pleasing in experiences is connection with the spirit,
Writing a nice letter is like an inner walk,
How putting colours in a painting makes the day shine,
Playing with animals is listening to the heart,
To live is to cultivate the moment where yesterday says goodbye,
Putting water on a plant is to be able to feel its smile,
You do not have to choose the best in how happy the enigma is.

EXIT THE MASK

Among other people's glances there are different visions,
The distances with reflections wear masks,
In intrepid interpretations the image speaks,
The person represents the footprint in the resonance,
In adaptation the personality is disguised,
Where in societies there are theatrical characters,
Identity restricted by feigning inauthentic ways,
Necessity is coexistence by the matrix creator,
The social is the program by the rules to respect,
Wise adaptation is a tool of opportunities,
Social molds embellish under fragile features,
The shadow of the opposite pole is hiding the public,
The figures restore with achievements in interpretation,
Reality must be flexible to social browsing,
Pain and wear awaits align artificial adaptation,
Repress the external with internal in logic drowns,
The box of surprises in his days will open,
There are mysteries that grow but are not reality,
Sowing doubts is an old mind game,
The rejected contents are saved to the unconscious,
The instructions of time open in ways,
When recovering life with efforts they unbalance,
Finding the riddle is a constant equilibrium,
Rigidity is endangered by separating the union from the self,
There are coded dialogues with telepathic evolution,
The cultivation of the heart is fed without interest,
The blind is fanciful like a playground,
Protecting yourself is putting yourself in the right command,
Feeling peace illuminates shadows of the soul.

SIXTH SUN

Four corners that shine in equal intensity,
Geological changes on earth without going back,
Ignoring the existence of evil does not bring protection,
Years of confusion and doubt you greed with death,
Whoever wears humility finds wisdom,
A dialogue with the eternal knowledge,
Ancient suns that rule our galaxy,
The search for nowhere is in the meeting,
A distraction with work and debt makes us sleepy,
The rootless light will attract other extraterrestrial beings,
Knowledge hardens with religion and news,
Enraged science awakens in a flower,
Among trees and mountains some children smile,
The wonder of the creator is not an accident,
The magical dawn has mysterious keys,
By ignoring the ghost of evil, fanaticism is in danger,
Greed flows into the fire of swords,
The cracks of the pedestal opens to shine justice,
The will of love is embodied in enchanting,
The religion of fear ends between long dresses,
The crown of eternity is nameless and endless,
In the elevation of the eternal we are all gods,
The first thought is like a lamp
A genie appears to create the dream of emotion,
The law of gravity will always act when called,
The eyes in the sky search for lost calls,
A landscape with encryption gives a meaning to evolution,
The sacred tablets are the chronicles of progress,
The crew members will be interior advisers.

WARS ON MARS

In new horizons the battle crosses corners,
The between changes are the secrets in abduction,
Forced transfers for labor,
Slavery of Martians and Humanoids,
For corporations of reptilian and gray origin,
Leaders of the earth aware of reality,
Interstellar information hidden from humanity,
Very oppressive claws from Orion are raised,
Decades in abuses in need of Freedom,
The council of andromeda for collaboration,
Galactic Alliance enters with armed groups,
Space war with means in determination,
Control of invaders is the power of intervention,
Among regressive races, telepathy will be a mechanism,
Reptiles among insectoids in independent actions,
The manipulation and lethargy must stop submission,
Refusing to follow the condition roller to the target,
Stop oppression from the burrows of the elite,
The fortress must open the gates of the underworld,
Regressive bug escapes will be installed on Mars,
Shelter on Mars is a perfect plan cornered,
Radiation in chaos is rebuilt in worlds,
Photons of gamma light awaken regressive planes,
The rebellion of secret programs in rebellion,
Parallel cleaning search between moon and earth,
By the triangular points of endless power,
The threat in the galaxy is the greatest danger,
Getting connected is the acclaimed dimension,
The collective consciousness must unite a linear time.

DIMENSIONAL PORTAL

They say the laws of the universe are love,
The roads between closed doors open,
The traces of bad and sad surroundings hurt,
Where are the conditions looking for Freedom,
The imposed loads cut off the light inputs,
With deep cracks in pounding abysses,
Inside the dream there are openings with sounds,
The enigma of physics is a momentous mystery,
As in every morning there is a matrix awakening,
Medication is the unit of the spiritual reflex,
Hidden instincts change like instruments,
Cultivating positive thoughts is a sign of cleanliness,
How to find a fantastic story in each child,
To understand vibrations is to understand the soul,
Plans and circus strategies with distractions,
The manipulation is slow in the demonstrations,
In each graduate there is the aspiration of progress,
Among clear skies the navigation is smooth,
The galactic rays will shine on souls,
The universal mission is a project of liberation,
Planetary intervention is in authorised cycles,
The divine plan brings advertising beginnings,
Very rare landings for guests,
Between walks the contacts will be accentuated,
The explorations will conduct command ships,
Extra galactics will come to instruct with technology,
Motherships with extensive flights for visits,
In the apparent there are realities to clean toxins,
Advanced secret technologies will be shared.

LIGHT IN THE DARKNESS

Genius is the inspiration to excel,
In the darkness there are creative windows,
Where there is patience there is value in harmony,
The value in each one is reference guide,
Impotence are insecure diagnoses,
A Benedict is the assurance of progress,
With forecasts without ties or haste,
The cricket cage is the dangerous warning,
The inner teacher is sentimental emotion,
In the attitude are the molecular receptors,
Enthusiasm and discouragement activate realities,
Reconciliation is creative inner freedom,
Your own hatred can be your own prisoner,
There are mental messages that alter reactions,
Confidence is the invention of the spiritual future,
The gift of a flower is a fantasy of emotion,
Making the soul bloom is an eternal garden,
It is written in the shadow of the underworld chants,
Energy aid with orientation reflections,
A critical mass must awaken in volume,
In different pipelines the direction is indirect,
Telepathic and very psychically structural,
Dreams of laughter are healing of life,
Body and soul united is the best gift of freedom,
Being different reaches the inner gaze,
Guilty do not exist the extraordinary life is in you,
What you give returns the harvest is an echo of your heart,
Like a childhood friend in simple conversation,
In years without existence there is transit without death.

THE HUMAN FARM

Invisible manipulation will be inevitable,
Armies with clones of laboratories will arrive,
Similar to androids their reliable programs,
Military servants with keys to the great silence,
An entity without light covering the economy,
Among directed programs beings are chosen,
Altered dictators difficult to identify,
The triumph of control will fall into spiritual fear,
What is hidden in obstacles awakens in knowledge,
A cosmic awakening is the basis of a new gospel,
The intellectual surprise will be a creative mold,
Fanatic frequencies emitted by waves,
Believing addicts crawling into the abyss
Master assumptions fed by control,
Rituals of energies using pain in shades,
Sadomasochistic vibes with evil tune,
Deceptions by the soaring poisoned intrepid,
Inner identities with voids in the senses,
Innocent humans lost in dark forces,
The portal of lies is to sell the kingdom of heaven,
Entities of the astral with satisfaction of searches,
The distance in search is like a human farm,
By invaders who impose repetitive doctrines,
To dominate the dragon is to be reborn from vices,
The remnant man is resurrected rising,
The great sign from heaven will be the radiance of stars,
The great march is to populate and fertilise new land,
Like the courage and will of a majestic bird,
With a flash of light an infinite path is born.

THE UNBEATABLE POWER

A supreme organism of the reborn interior,
Connection is the only sacred way of elevation,
The eternal creator leads to development without distraction,
Between yoga and technical stretching confuse,
Wisdom with intelligence falls from heaven,
Simple conversations that come from the heart,
Only in the silence of meditation do works appear,
The reflection of each condition is to fix errors,
The path in consciousness is led with love,
The interplanetary day elders guiding,
The taste of truth is shared honesty,
Check is intact law to historical reality,
Blind guides purifying the outside of the cup,
Blind guides with filth within,
The generation of vipers will be fleeting,
The fearless warrior unveils the truth,
Gods of revel-ion with cults for domains
Slave populations from the top of pyramids,
They pay tribute with unjust sacrifices to satisfy,
The moment of symbols by imaginary presence,
The followers of worship come with an end to the method,
The impulse of transit strips the material,
Iron legs with Jewish leaders,
The executing arm loses control over powers,
Ruling industries put world delusions,
The perfect plan has an end in time,
Large lands will be opened to benefit shelters,
Getting rid of burdens is survival gain,
Preserving life in consciousness of love.

YOUR MIND TRANSFORMS THE BODY

Between the double slits levels form the quantum,
The interference pattern is the key in waves,
Observing masters transform treasures,
Great brilliants are comparative experiences,
The process is a support like columns,
Passion implies enthusiasm for the goal,
Between successes with joys, choices are created,
Obstacles are overcome by compromising,
To overcome dreams knowledge is achieved,
Repetition makes the impossible possible,
Every human being is a sculptor of his celebration,
Peace and serenity is the voice that helps the soul,
While the outside listening overrides the target,
Attitude are cellular chemical processes,
Excessive discouragement is the enemy of spirit,
Some footprints in disguise sow loneliness,
New ideas are like shaky floors,
Roots of progress are wrapped in changes,
The imagination of structures is a journey,
Where there is transformation there is cunning,
Safety is the pleasure of good behaviour,
How dancing in the rain is unicorn magic,
When you enjoy solitude you talk to the Interior,
How to talk to plants is to understand life,
Take care of the human sigh that falls into eternal sleep,
As each one is the result is in the acts,
The craftsman of the body connects the mind to the soul,
Between the old memory love is reborn again,
Enjoying the short life transforms everything into beauty.

HIDDEN DOORS

The fall of the sun is a dialogue united with the sea,
To love in oblivion is child rebirth,
Welcome the life that continues in death,
In calls of key mysteries they carry jumps,
If freedom is free, why live as a slave,
I am not the way but the one who causes it,
I face the enemy to know about the past,
He who accepts a compliment begins to be dominated,
In concentration serenity lights up,
It is not wise to judge without first being looked at,
Between verses and verses there is sacred company,
Ceremonies with prayers is the worst dictator,
Between notes of sounds there is joy and hope,
In salvation is the testimony of oneself,
Surrender implies knowing how to flow in new ways,
Rowing against the current does not advance the changes,
Problems come to teach to walk a shortcut,
The victims have no power to assume their life,
Real love is what they give you without asking,
A awake person does not try to change anyone,
By opening your mind and heart you see yourself,
True peace is controlling torments,
The ego exhausts the walker because it always seeks,
Molecules dissolve to shine again,
The beginning and the end is creation of the mind,
When you feel that you are not what you think you will fly,
The opportunity is every day for eternity,
Art is a fable of beauty without borders,
In learning to live, our whole lives are lost.

FROM JAIL TO HOME

An elite forgets human commandments,
Justice is harmony in inequality,
A serious illness is a bell,
It is not born only of the mother but also when it is found,
To be born is to realise who you really are,
Man owns what he loves and enjoys,
As the mind is a slave to what it thinks,
Lions do not refuse to applaud a tiger,
The library is a learning paradise,
As life without music is a sleeping Eden
Courage is saying what money doesn't buy,
Feeling the earth ignites contact with differences,
Between knowledge, history will be reborn,
Fear is a dictator if you don't chase dreams,
The scars of work is not knowing how to live life,
Much on the outside and nothing on the inside is cheating,
Distracting conditions are doors to jail,
The hero is not confused when reaching symphony,
Exhausting the mind is in separating the roots,
Risking is profit from objective battles,
He who loses everything serenely wins everything on the way,
Calm nature puts flowers on thorns,
Take care of the steps that you climb will be the same as you descend,
Rico is the one who needs the least in his destiny,
Drowning for material is unnecessary sacrifice,
Leave curiosity I took you where the destiny hero goes,
Life is beautiful danger when you trust his game,
Starting at every moment is the task of growth,
The light of the infinite is united with the works.

THE GALACTIC NIGHT

The protection of skies will be light activation,
The rise of glaciers will be rainbow colours,
By removing training roots they lose control,
The animals will be ex jumped so as not to run,
Under something meek and obedient a void crosses,
A solar track hanging by a thread in transition,
A challenge will move sands into deserts,
Meditation is reborn and progresses in destiny,
Helping will be success under humanitarian control,
The dark will reduce its power amid disappointments,
Systems failure falls due to explosive efforts,
The seals of Revelation nears the exchange,
The breath of the times is like a snake,
An end of cycles is balanced with intuitions,
Astrology is adapted by twelve expansions,
When not understanding words, silence is admired,
Like a gearbox only carries movements,
The separate streams will be closed,
Flames of fire in mountains sigh,
A labyrinth of time is guessing dangers,
Resource drops are keys to infinity,
A critical point terrifies the second awakening,
The creator will be the potential of the future virgin,
The land will be cultivated by the restored forest,
Thought is retarded by not using feelings,
Between a book the meditation jewels are born,
The prolongation of the juvenile process is real,
The balance between the answer will be evolution,
Among the old a book will have a new history.

ALIEN INTERVENTION

The light codes for a global awakening,
Taking control enhances the image of spells,
The success of each one is part of the whole,
Prophecy is used as psychological on a bridge,
The power play is in the trained consciousness,
When knowing a lot, doubts interfere,
Each one is the head of the symphony that lives,
The energies method will be renewable upon understanding,
Trapped dependency is incapacity,
Any salvation is in the search for a solution,
To be a victim is to live in sleeping confusion,
Teachers feel when something hurts
By stopping the mind the source of life is analysed,
A principle of alpha and omega is universal,
The doors of time stop to analyse themselves,
Punishing feelings steal peace,
The doubling in meditation is necessary,
The invisible creators bring wisdom,
A rebellion will be a springboard for progress,
Temporary openings recover without escapes,
A fallen angel will be the source of the new creation,
A divine mystery will be certainty in the eternal,
Survival exploration will bring a guide,
The reign will be the accessible Resurrection,
A new age will stabilise disorder,
Finding the questions is feeling the balance,
The past must be compatible with the present,
Being reborn is more important than solving problems,
A united and admirable harmony of thought will come.

THE SEVEN EXPLOSIONS

The seventh seal of Revelation unmasked,
A zodiacal code between selected Kings,
Parasitic creatures take abandoned reins,
Mad minds return the crowns,
Epidemics and plagues are swept away by weariness,
The first spring branches are reborn,
Where the solar storm opens the cracks,
Like a bottle sailing in the infinite sea,
It carries a message between fresh and cold waters,
A cycle of unfolding has a beginning and an end,
The seven explosions joining past and future,
From indigo darkness and solutions shine,
The famous demons will fall by instinct,
For wanting to be a conqueror, roots are lost,
Strength never wins, love has always won,
Among catastrophes, consciousness is danger,
Jerusalem invaded by armies with false futures,
The footprint of the sphinx arrives with signs of the sun,
In errors there is no wisdom if there is no understanding,
The end of the cycle recalls the deluge of past gods,
There are levels of paralysis to be cleared,
Flying objects will be invasions,
Between obstacles there are distractions from greed,
Due to distrust the purification is delayed,
The energies are raised by the updated interior,
A cure is the change of thought,
The puppets of sin hide freedom,
Imposing ideas takes away the progress of the soul,
The awakening enriches seeking understanding.

A NEW MAN

A fulfilment in full development and progress,
Among the darkness the inner truth is sought,
Knowledge is not belief, it is logic,
The condition is the will of constancy,
A final time will bloom in the beginning of the truth,
New leader is the birth of dull love,
The mission of the astrals is in superior beings,
Traveler's of light will open the next hope,
The levels of the universe open without hiding places,
Intuitive shadows rise to fulfilment,
There are challenges with answers of the time that ends,
The cultures of heaven are gods with footprints,
Without worship consciousness understands wisdom,
The superior culture understands mutual respect.
The falls of order in fanaticism disappear,
The central sun is a hidden science of the universe,
Peace does not depend on the vicissitudes or religious,
The laws of faith are old but they sleep,
Between corners the knowledge is the same,
Other forces transformed lethal information,
There are very clear missions and with curative development,
Masters are using transference and wisdom,
Leaders to guide the spirit of the sleeping being,
Examples include enigmas,
Reincarnation always resonates helping,
The special purpose is a gift to share,
Consciousness is not unlimited in illusion,
As the stones feel in the height of rocks,
Writing tests take lessons from time.

THE APPOINTMENT OF THE COVENANT

Messengers of the world of cosmic brotherhood,
Yesterday and today will unite between fallen angels,
The elevation would be noticed in energetic atoms,
An agency will sink for the corrupt future,
Prayer chains won't change paths,
Disobedience to the government is to survive power,
Bright birds will approach the dark world,
The embrace of ideas in union is the healing key,
There are frequencies of force that will be crews,
Higher commands will calm fury,
At the end of the horizon there are hopes of progress,
The voyages of new days approach the sea,
Images with chicken wings collapse,
Knowledge is spiritual legacy in prophecies,
A transverse axis is transparent in matter,
Nation against nations will destroy kingdoms,
The queen of the south would rise in a new dawn,
The sons of perdition will fall from storms,
The four powers are submerged under a secret,
The ancient of times appear in destruction,
The signs of doom will calm screams,
Sin is the impostor of implantation,
The same strength will be reborn underfoot,
A crown dressed as the sun with moon and stars
The symbols of light do not need to see or hear,
Humility will be able to decode feelings,
A birthing belt will give birth,
The dragon of darkness will fall into a hole,
The vices of anguish will be devoured.

THE OLD MAN OF THE DAYS

The crown from the supreme universal creation,
The mystery of eternal life is the tree,
Among the cycles the enigmas are the beings,
Where nothingness and passivity are concentrated,
Among the spheres the I am is divine consciousness,
With the breath the word is like the wind,
A magician with the splendour of wise tricks,
The suns bathe the universe with their light every day,
The spirit of the cloud-dwelling dew shines,
As the sand is from the sea, the desert is from the sand,
A labyrinth is the pause in search of the way,
As a cult is led by a leader for the lost,
Between dark dungeons sentences tremble,
Fanaticism is malicious dishonour,
Individual instrument as en masse catches,
Between statues the magic sleeps in cults,
Where strategies use the symbol for praise,
Discreet manipulation comes from old days,
Where faith subdues men in the invisible,
The art of books supports freedom of expression,
The invaders face free will,
The sown seed is the formula of the universe,
Among the matrix the symbols are zodiacal,
Breaking barriers is the career without an interpreter,
Hidden values must be found,
By using energies in positive keys it is repaired,
A substance rises and experiences joys,
Inner knowledge is the source of wisdom,
Where the signals open sleeping minds.

THE BEST VACCINE

Waves and eternal wind sound among the seas,
It is chemistry in harmony with inner peace,
The substance is elevated for days awake,
The creative power of the body is its intelligence,
The heart beats for the spirit runs healing,
Chromosomes read DNA by sensors,
Among experiences is the next order,
Gratitude is the love of infinity with sparkles,
Songs are wrapped in the earth with the body,
Genes and proteins produce antibodies,
Between the interior of the mountains there is life,
Through the veins of the human you can see the roots,
Tied by the stars are the levels,
All balance is the frequency of the environment,
As a cyclist is fixed in his race and turned,
Putting a plan in contact is to unite intelligence,
We are all interior potential design,
Mind body is the atom between quantum space,
Biological change is the cause of the effect,
The circuits is the driving force behind the experience,
The neocortex is the little nut of learning,
The power that created the body can heal,
Between circuits emotions create stars,
The second limbo brain are controlling actions
The knowledge experience is in the mind,
While the authorities are for the body,
It is the arrival of the sincere leader's compassion,
Evolution is three free steps,
Continuously review and remember.

THE TRUST

Where the day hides the eternal stars,
In deep knowledge without being perfect,
Keys on keyring with keys to bridges,
Where when crossing mysteries there are steps and shadows,
Courage without a map is choosing choices,
Wayfarer with principles drags his divine faith,
The impulses are empires in the inner union,
We are not what limitations impose systems,
It is thoughts that put limitations,
Thinking what we are not obscures the beauty,
Touching the deep night comes the dimension,
Hearing the call steps go forward,
In a black hole there is loss of energy,
When opening to infinity the brain is molded,
Valuing moments is a visual illusion approach,
Creating the future is training the positive mind,
The reflection looks inside between silences,
Creativity is creating a playing field,
Where is the magic to new opportunities,
Passion is the lever of creative motive,
Commitment is determination of trust,
The range of colours is the courage of the moment,
Remember the inner greatness is to collect the self,
Under the forces of progress there are emotions,
The past informs but does not determine defeats,
A diagnosis process leads to prognosis,
But the Benedict is the freedom of being and soul,
The cage of crickets is the jailer of the spirit,
While the inner master decides his goal.

WITHOUT LIMITS

In inspiration there is part of the universe,
Where the root is the emotional richness,
Following the footsteps are efforts to hopes,
By emptying losses, novelties are enriched,
The spirit flies to live in the present,
The ramparts are a game with a crew,
Between ties the past weighs like old age,
In the presences of the moment the now shines,
The voices inside understand each other in silence,
Spontaneous smiles are refreshed,
Responding to reason confuses clarity,
Opportunistic explanations keep peace away,
Reaction is a compulsion mechanism,
Power is natural funny easy movement,
Stopping to manipulate you will be manipulated,
The tranquility transforms thorns into flowers,
Contemplate first to act later,
Closing circuits every moment is surmountable,
In eternity love speaks through everything
The artificial distracts the essential from progress,
The attention of the whole are rivers in libraries,
Among the museums are monasteries,
How do they listen? Animals are like plants,
The body follows the order of the mind without measures,
Honesty is the sacredness of a temple,
With serenity everything becomes light,
The true company is sublime and purifies,
Connection with oneself is in the heart,
The moment is the objective and the goal.

ANCESTRAL SNAKE

Wise and awake governor,
Traveler of the hidden in nightmares,
Subconscious of the spine,
Spy of the human in his sleeping turns,
Sculptor of myths with the force awake,
The chants of mantras attract the information,
Philosophical basis of the stomach image,
Beauty of the earth connected to the brain,
Union of wisdom attentively to the environment,
The ancient healing power in sculpture,
With image of value from the human psyche,
Contingent value between quicksand,
Song painting between collective dreams,
Union of the deep trance of the unconscious,
The truth of spirit traits in colours,
Earth-walker immersed in the hidden,
Under the ayahuasca ceremonies it interferes,
From the amazon river with the magic drawn,
The anaconda under its mantle navigates the water,
Air and earth united in nature birth,
United soul among the icaros of time,
Ayahuasca the yage mother of all plants,
Impulses of truth in galactic ceremonies,
Fountain of peace in sacred harmonies,
Between life the liana stem connects,
History is reborn in the sleeping spirit,
I walk DMT fire between awakened senses,
Through the serpent of fear the spirit is reborn,
Collared mirror for divine healing.

WORLD REBELLION

The lion will roar for changes in mankind,
A white light seals the earth with its veil,
The divine force is in faith with hope,
Between mountains the ships will be raised,
A set is divided but is inseparable,
The starlight will unite the footprints in minds,
There are armies that will tremble on the earth,
Where the truth is revealed between the curtains,
There will be broken pieces still between prostheses,
The protection will be to prevent nuclear access,
Under talents resources will be trapped,
In the great nation there are children with intuition,
The beautiful and sweet energy comes from the spirit,
Between silences the changes will be radical,
From heaven the signs will illuminate life,
Religious falls will see abysses unchanged,
The life economist will hang between rungs,
Between tears the cries of the sea hide,
A rebellion to deworm is gleaming,
The power for slavery will fall into misery,
From the trials souls will be delivered,
Where there are endings between hidden attempts,
Separations are inevitable in this regard,
The light is born in the darkness for the origin,
From the swamps the ashes will be cleaned,
A rebirth comes for the truth of the whole,
Teachings are imposed for the needy,
Progress is feeding the soul with happiness,
Reborn slowly at the end of love.

RESPONSIBLE FOR AWAKENING

You do not know what you have, until you lose it,
Reality arises by adapting again,
Transforming consciousness is quality of calm,
The greatest enemies are thoughts,
Where circumstantial forms are created,
Judgments are the food to live reflexes,
In spirituality lives the love of the soul,
Animals are our teachers,
As in plants there is metamorphosis,
Living is the key to continue in happiness,
A good learning avoids looking at other people's faults,
The heart is the intuitive reason for the connection,
When you think you know all the answers,
The universe arrives and changes all the questions,
Any loss is gain to understand,
The heart speaks from sentimental emotion,
The blind mind between passions never listens,
Speech repeats experiences between traps,
Silences free while the soul slept,
By investing in talent, the breath is impregnated,
Being and not appearing is the key to finding peace,
Doing is the power of saying which one elevates the self,
To have wisdom is not to accuse anyone,
Sickness is the way to wake up,
Forgiveness is not forgetting, it is remembering without pain,
Sharing wise teachings is knowing how to love,
Humour is the means to change the world,
Like a flower leaves its petals in light and breezes,
To reborn the seas among its beautiful brilliance.

THE STAR SHADOWS

A polar poem speaking in another language,
A galaxy with mysteries and hidden missions,
The dimensions are nature in flashes,
Time lines between mantras food,
The inner change is the awakening from DNA,
Between disunity souls are created divided,
From rebellion in need power is lost,
Between technology with hidden time travel,
The manipulated manifestation is by an order,
Knowledge brings change with protection,
Do not take the ice that sleeps the walker,
There is a junction with a transition point,
A connection of the stars united with firm steps,
Between heaven and earth springs reflect,
The secret of history awakens the sleeping grave,
Behind the sun there is a planet of origin,
The reptilian Anunnaki are evolutionary progress,
The constellation arrivals protect,
The water carries the sailor among the waves of the sea,
Traces of gold are left over when they dazzle from the sun,
Feeling the earth ignites contact with the heart,
When writing from the soul energies are purified,
An Iberian protection will bring increase and capacity,
Blue flowers and carats help to raise success,
A horizon is a union of upper and lower case letters,
Since radiation is fractional particles,
A plane of movement will be a figure of the alphabet,
The address in languages are derived from the whole,
The essential thing is the reach of means without limits.

DISGUISED AGENDA

The identity of inverted seas in words,
In civil disobedience tyrannies protest,
The depopulation agenda is to sterilise,,
Killer human reduction from economics,
Scientific false alleged global warming,
Pollution the perfect poison of pain,
Selective world spread out for the young,
Social unrest for a nuclear start,
Obligation injected passport is to get vaccinated,
Platforms are networks for spectrum,
Slide silent resistors lock,
Ruthless resignation has no escape,
The executioner saviours mislead the shortcut,
The bright future is blindly imagined,
Distrust operates in arguments,
Acceding in resistance is a dark scene,
The intentions are to cover the mouth, eyes and ears,
Potential weapons are imposed on peoples,
Police and politicians is perverse manipulation,
Instruments are not justified in tyrannies,
The blind magic raises the future in Freedom,
In the jail house the waves of the sea rise,
With subjugations they catch summers in pain,
Psychopaths use psychological force,
It's a chain of hostages in full swing,
Sacrifice will be the motto that raises order,
Protests will be inevitable for freedom,
Fight for Health is to fight Satanism,
Disobedience is the perfect plan to live.

SLAVE PROGRAM

Necessity is the key to slavery,
Human beings are divided between minds,
Time in overcrowded devastated land,
A utopian mission conquers equality,
Opposite worlds did the spatial and terrestrial,
Balance is taking the reins calmly,
Three parables at the end of the judgment sound,
The talents of nations are managements,
Between dimensions the food is grown,
Inner success develops with serving,
Legions wrap themselves in a crown of thorns,
The celestial mechanics opens with success,
Between the orbits reality is the key,
Invisible winters space stations,
Reconquests are born amidst pollution,
Spatial rules are prices without destination,
Control in disobedience with electrons,
Zero tolerance is the perfect plan,
Earth pollutes between command metals,
Impositions separating minds,
There are borders with radar ships,
Radiation is the virus that traps,
In the implanted codes are the laws,
The protocol is for effect on differences,
The real is not received by reason, only reality,
Training delivers lost strength,
In creativity is the game of wisdom,
Illusion is the hope of the afterlife,
Evaluation of the process is harmony.

OPPOSITE POLES

An extraordinary ordinary is a hero,
Seas with names without being separated,
Feeding the trapped roots to the program,
Life system designed for the happy blind,
Time with pacemaker in a hurry with no way out,
TV shows designed with strategies,
Fear of secrets to lock up trash,
Spectrum set with invisible colours,
Society of doom to love fast,
Continuous processor on submissive brains,
Consciousness off for the lost announcer,
Conscious in narrow frequency bands,
The subconscious of the infinite isolated from being,
Reality of care for a small world,
Tournament race for separate nations,
Search understanding without knowing who you are,
Identity thoughts invested in words,
Rain of the panorama prepared to limitations,
The encryption has a key without disconnections,
The decoder is the enigma to the target,
The form is an apprenticeship for a new kingdom,
Between time and sky, sea and land is DNA,
Environmental electrons carry air,
Sense of emotions is a manipulable process,
Concern for progress is the main theme,
The government game is a bloody road,
Vibration is united by calming restrictions,
Good chess of life when perceived is activated,
The level becomes visible by imagining the top.

NURSES OF HONOUR

Key of sacrifices consecrated in silent triumphs,
With an oil lamp heroes soldiers in battles,
With their valuable gifts they give away treasures of harmony,
Between the nights and days some footprints leave art,
From professional hands there are unsigned pictures,
The value is very immense, some hide tears,
Some seagulls look out and scream from windows,
In its streams of steps energies are kept,
With secret hugs surrounds patience to the spirit,
In corners are drawn hands that do not separate races,
Some seeds are sown where the soul flourishes,
Every work by each artist has an honour award,
The price is unimaginable for being painters of the universe,
In stars eternal appreciable smiles shine,
From deep transformation songs will return them,
Hawks carry voices remembering the anonymous, painter,
Diamonds from forgotten drops in the universe shine,
Observed from infinity they are polished with light,
The divine envelops them like well-polished paintings,
Their voices sound like medicines that repair wounds,
The image of artists is continuously in their work,
The encounter with the whole admires the brave nurse,
The universal law envelops the hearts of effort,
Without judging the sky, they etch fluorescent roots,
When memories open, the magic of caresses shines,
Sacred people of the world offering blessings,
They are the plants of the eternal with unforgettable aromas,
They are the most precious jewels attached to the universe,
Nurses are colour of hopes and respect for life.

ARTIFICIAL SYSTEM

A playing force is infiltrated in decisions,
Literally destiny is to be a connection to the artificial,
Humans have no creative spark or will of their own,
Kidnapping from other worlds is the key to obedience,
Reestablishing judgment is far to come in darkness,
The beginning of care is the trap door,
Internal core of the world order is not 100% human,
Defending Freedom is the basis of awakening from obedience,
There are nets for the soul with recycling traps,
Reincarnation is necessary the light is on hold,
From consciousness there is an optional opportunity,
Worry traps the soul in pain for deception,
The disquieting gloom seeks for free thinkers,
There are dark burrows for someone else's conspiracy,
Beyond this planet where suppression comes,
Layers of geo engineering corruption are illuminate,
With agendas for UFO radiation and interests,
Alien intervention for genetic abductions,
Sources of repression in exchange interceptions,
Suppress ideas of knowledge with plans to convince,
Search for gears to serve as machines,
Non-physical entities feed on sad energies,
Shadows of mud are erased and recycled for returns,
Prison planet a crawl field by not waking up,
Batteries food symbols for not losing fears,
Hidden forces generate strategies with grace,
The consents with light follow blind courses,
Forces are systems, you just have to remember who you are,
Protect yourself in being convertible to synthetic ideas.

BORN AGAIN

Some fluorescent kites leave fleeting messages,
Life teaches that everything you want you cannot have,
Life teaches first is to enjoy what you already have,
Life teaches that a wound can make us stronger,
Life teaches that pain is not forever,
Life teaches the sorrows do not annihilate to defeat,
Life teaches suffering, only character is better forged,
Life teaches that loneliness is not bad and has a good end,
Life teaches that losing yourself is more worse,
Life teaches failures are part of learning,
Life teaches that without falls no changes are known,
Life teaches not to please everyone for fear of losing them,
Life teaches that sow good is to grow with the universe.
Life teaches if the past returns that you do not answer it,
Life teaches when you return you have nothing new to say,
Life teaches what they think of you does not define who you are,
Life teaches your current situation does not define your end,
Life teaches thinking a lot only unnecessarily exhausts,
Life teaches that it is better to focus on possibilities,
Life teaches that we are all fighting a battle,
Life then teaches to be kind to each other,
Life teaches if there are plans that fail let them go,
Life teaches that your dreams never leave them,
Life teaches don't judge your neighbour tries to understand,
Life teaches take care of who you meet when climbing,
Life teaches that always you will go down the same ladder,
Use your smile to change sadness in the world,
Don't let the world change your smile for sorrow,
Silent looks involve power and respect.

SLAVES TO ENSLAVE

A seer world living blind in wait,
While the medicine advances the disease too,
There are actions with dissimulation for objectives of interests.
Keep doing what has always been done is the key,
Demolishing to be able to replace novelties is a ruse,
Where each problem created already has a solution,
The system is a cult without borders for obligations,
Food to survive is the strategy of the game,
The oppression of the system is to feel fear to obey,
To get out of punishment is to find the essence of the truth,
Observation is enough to know the movement,
Effort implies tension where attention is powerful,
In a state of non-resistance, circumstances change,
To improve it is necessary not to attend to the challenges,
Surrender comes when you stop asking questions
Happiness and unhappiness are varying waves.,
Success in life is in the quality that you label it,
In the light itself the flame of the spirit becomes visible,
Peace is the supreme current in constant melody,
Only the noise of the constant mind becomes obstacles,
Collective mental patterns are heavy layers,
We run out of the present to visualize the future,
Suffering is not finding the point of union with the past,
The encounter with the self begins in silence with the whole,
I am past.
The free mind tied to time is like a prison.
I am present.
Life is dying before dying and finding yourself.
I am future.
Suffering is necessary until you realize it is unnecessary.
I am moment.
Where beyond time there is no reality.
The light fades the darkness.

THE DOSSIER BOX

On the edge of reality the best moments are simple,
While the gazes become seagulls in the air they fly,
It gets late between laughter and tears life is gone,
The moon lights up when the soul falls in love,
The flowers are named after the glittering mountains,
The fire is lit and the wood burns with life,
Between the seas fires will burn sweeping away water,
From the earth roots will rise between good and evil,
The mother will empty her womb and it will be time to visualise,
The believer will no longer believe the atheist is the believer,
The tears will be an echo between downpours of screams,
The wind with hurricanes will bring a punishment from heaven,
The wall built by human slaves will be cleaned,
Only when the noise ends an emptiness will sit,
In the end the pain will be seen with the same eyes in harmony,
The feelings will sing with memories of strength,
A cross will scream awakening to free understanding,
Observing in the infinite the light of the inner universe,
Among white arrows with seeds of learning,
An encounter with the whole takes the origin by the hand,
Looking for order in appearance to correct,
The delusions are of the trials without exits to be valued,
Roots on the heights form the firmament,
Chemistry only attracts distracts the target in challenges,
Alchemy integrates the principle transform and visualise,
In conclusion alchemy brings together what chemistry separates,
What the human knows is a drop and what the human does not know is
the ocean,
Only a gift from a story says there is no tomorrow,
They will be newly constructed with different writings history.

THE ALARM SOUNDS

This weakened generation believing in softness,
Where they see everything offensive including the truth,
They will drag their tears awakening in their currents,
The cracks will be felt to recognise their falls,
Between needles of sides the thoughts do not breathe,
The devil's trick is to make believe without much convincing,
Between hidden roots the silence is interpreted with noise,
Chemical killers - biological successfully suffocate,
The plagues walking among the clouds and the winds,
Sowing poison in animals and fields by dressing,
Diseases with sores on dying bodies,
The capsule is launched without respecting pacts they create enemies,
The world goes dumb as molten lead melts,
Their flesh will fall before they break their knees,
No one hears or sees hunger and without justice it approaches,
The darkness of the dragon seemed to sleep but the bear awakens,
Terror seems humble but harbours dark poverty,
The cup has overflowed it is no longer possible to turn back,
The atomic arrives without a solution, the third call will explode,
Fall from the sky with the slag-clad crew,
The nation rises where earthquakes seek principles,
The sun goes out among the plague that swallowed a few years,
The proud without restraint will no longer be able to caress his vices,
Religions will fall with capitalism and politics,
The moment will speak will lift the spirit in new peace,
A colony in the highlands will be the refuge of the materialised,
The reborn light just shines in hope,
In the unexpected the illumination of the shadows will return,
Power is to get up to flourish and improve every day.

THE PARADISE OF THE RENAISSANCE

Life is the choice between the truth and the lie,
Paradise is never lost it is only forgotten with distractions,
In a lost eternity you can start again,
To stop looking in the mirror is to learn to swim inside,
With face to the sun walking and with the moon flying,
For what is not seen what is essential happens that we see,
Among the calm breeze rivers reflect the blowing clouds,
The landscapes between them hide with the shadows,
The flavour stays with life in inner harmony,
The smell lost in days is strange with waiting,
Where the image is oblivion the external puts beliefs,
Words are voices that are heard with echoes,
Among the invisible of the beginning is born with the formation of the
fetus,
Only the visibility is frontal with the hidden image,
On the back we are chased by the armour that transforms,
Experienced expression finds meaning,
Emotional wounds spread through family ties,
Until someone conscious stops the pattern process,
The changes are necessary to avoid repeating programs,
All fatigue has a beginning with a limit,
In solar energy an eclipse hides brilliance and power,
From nothing there is perfection with the spirit of the universe,
Offering the blessing of enjoying knowing how to share,
Saving the unnecessary is a fierce enemy imaginable,
Where by swallowing the whole the end is to stop or destroy oneself,
Only by acquiring wisdom do footprints have shapes,
Forms are the keys to universal understanding,
Where rebirth writes progress constantly,
To leave the invisible in the visible of the eternal paradise

Printed in the United States
by Baker & Taylor Publisher Services